LIVE
LOVE BIGGER

"This book is a gorgeous read, a shot in the arm, and a balm for the weary soul! Kathryn Whitaker's writing is truly a gift. With honesty and hilarity, she shares her own struggles and leads us to deep insights that will touch our hearts and inspire us to be better wives, moms, and daughters of God. We are in this struggle together, and Kathryn Whitaker is our beloved Texan cheerleader, encouraging us with uncommon humility, wisdom, and grace."

Danielle Bean
Catholic author and brand manager of CatholicMom.com

"Kathryn Whitaker writes just likes she loves—with conviction! With sweet southern style she shares openly about her faith and fears, triumphs and trials of raising her Texas-sized family. *Live Big, Love Bigger* will leave you empowered to live a more authentic life by making space for a little more Jesus and a lot more love. BBQ sauce not included."

Kelli Kelley
Founder and CEO of Hand to Hold

"In *Live Big, Love Bigger*, Kathryn Whitaker invites us into the sacred story of her life with God, family, and friends. The birth of the Whitakers' son Luke called her to suffering, a more intimate relationship with God, and ultimately to a whole new life. Her story is one of dying to self in order to live for Christ and her husband, children, and friends. People of faith have influenced Whitaker; by her life and these reflections, she influences others and calls them to value family and grow in faith. Whitaker's story enables us to get in touch with our own sacred story and discover anew God's incredible love often shown by the other people he places in our lives."

Most Rev. Gregory Aymond
Archbishop of New Orleans

"In any real friendship, there comes a moment when a friend pours her heart out and shares the fears and painful experiences you never knew she was carrying. Kathryn Whitaker, the mom of six who has everything together on the outside, gives us the same intimate gift in her relatable and beautifully vulnerable journey of faith, family, and recovery from the lie that we can control the life God has planned for us. Like its author, *Live Big, Love Bigger* is warm, witty, and served with a side of southern sass."

Haley Stewart
Catholic blogger, podcaster, and author of *The Grace of Enough*

"With the tone of a friend sitting down with you for some BBQ and real talk, Kathryn Whitaker shows us how to dream big and keep our sanity in the process."

Jennifer Fulwiler
SiriusXM radio host and author of *One Beautiful Dream*

"Real, transparent, and inspiring, Kathryn Whitaker's vulnerability in sharing how her carefully constructed facade crumbled upon the premature birth of her son will help others lean into, rather than avoid, the curveballs of life. Reading this book is like rocking on a porch swing and chatting with your closest friend as your hidden struggles are met with deep encouragement."

Brandon Vogt
Content director of Word on Fire Catholic Ministries
and author of *Why I Am Catholic (and You Should Be Too)*

"If you believe that pursuing a faithful life is intimidating or overwhelming, I highly encourage you read this book. Whitaker's story, laden with numerous examples of God's ability to work miracles in our present day lives, is a raw, down-to-earth account of a woman seeking to follow God the best way she knows how. Whitaker takes off her mask to show you the real woman she is—hurts, flaws, mistakes, and all—and how, despite it all, she's been able to witness and be a part of God doing miraculous work in her heart and in our world."

Jenna Guizar
Founder of Blessed Is She

"You may think your own family is far from perfect, and perhaps have never considered them 'holy.' If so, then this book is for you."

From the foreword by **Fr. Dave Dwyer, C.S.P.**
Executive director of Busted Halo Ministries

LIVE BIG, LOVE BIGGER

★

GETTING REAL WITH BBQ, SWEET TEA, AND A WHOLE LOTTA JESUS

KATHRYN WHITAKER

Ave Maria Press   AVE   Notre Dame, Indiana

Founded in 1865, Ave Maria Press is a ministry of the United States Province of Holy Cross.

www.avemariapress.com

Paperback: ISBN-13 978-1-59471-914-1

E-book: ISBN-13 978-1-59471-915-8

Cover photograph by Shannon Cunningham Photography.

Cover background © gettyimages.com.

Cover and text design by Katherine Robinson.

Printed and bound in the United States of America.

Library of Congress Cataloging-in-Publication Data.
Names: Whitaker, Kathryn, author.
Title: Live big, love bigger : getting real with BBQ, sweet tea, and a
   whole lotta Jesus / Kathryn Whitaker.
Description: Notre Dame, IN : Ave Maria Press, 2019.
Identifiers: LCCN 2019018611 (print) | ISBN 9781594719141 (pbk.)
Subjects: LCSH: Whitaker, Kathryn. | Catholic women--United
   States--Biography.
Classification: LCC BX4705.W475 A3 2020 (print) | LCC BX4705.W475
(ebook)
   | DDC 282.092 [B]--dc23
LC record available at https://lccn.loc.gov/2019018611
LC ebook record available at https://lccn.loc.gov/2019981385

To Papa,
I love you more.

CONTENTS

FOREWORD

In the Catholic calendar, every year on the first Sunday after Christmas, we celebrate the Feast of the Holy Family of Jesus, Mary, and Joseph, or "Holy Family" for short. Often my preaching that day includes the disclaimer that there's a good reason we don't refer to it as the feast of the "perfect" family. For one thing, the scripture reading chosen by the Church for this day is the one where Mary and Joseph lose twelve-year-old Jesus in the temple . . . for three days! That sounds more like a scene from the movie *Little Miss Sunshine* than a divine lesson about the model family. (Remember the little girl standing at the gas station waiting patiently for the VW bus to swing back around and pick her up?) So, even when it comes to three of the holiest people we can think of—our Lord Jesus, his Blessed Mother, and St. Joseph—holiness does not equal perfection or some platonic ideal of family. Holy families can be messy, broken, prone to mistakes, and in need of redemption.

You may think your own family is far from perfect, and may have never considered them "holy." If so, then this book is for you. In the pages that follow, Kathryn Whitaker takes you on a journey with her holy family: a bumpy ride of emergency surgeries for a premature baby; a pilgrimage to find the best BBQ joint in Texas. Hers is an adventure of humility and grace, of being truly present to those you love as well as to those you meet along the way. Kathryn will set you on a "journey of holy purpose," as she calls it. "The destination is always important, but it's relationships along the way that change us."

I believe I am one of those "relationships along the way." I first got to know Kathryn years ago as a client for her graphic design business. She has tremendous talent and we instantly hit it off thanks to a common love of Dr Pepper. Lately though, I have become a big fan of her Instagram stories. Every morning I tap the little pink square on my phone to get my daily dose of someone who is *real*. These days, we have a lot of media that claims to be "reality this" or "reality that," but very little of it is what I would call real. Kathryn is real. Talking straight into the camera, oftentimes while hiding from the kids inside her walk-in closet, she genuinely and humorously shares her life with the world in thirty-second snippets of social media.

Similarly here, Kathryn bravely and honestly addresses the kinds of personal struggles and fears that most of us would shy away from even admitting to ourselves, let alone putting down in print for all to read. More important, we are challenged by her story. We are challenged to open our eyes to appreciate the "everyday holy," to see the presence of God not only in church but in the neonatal intensive care unit. It seems to me that most Catholics and Christians never quite get around to breaking down the artificial barriers between faith and everyday life. Kathryn takes a wrecking ball to those walls. And well she should! After all, Jesus doesn't ask us to follow him, think about him, love him for only one hour a week. "We forget that God is in the miracle business every day," she reminds us. And that's why she calls us to *Live Big, Love Bigger*.

One of my favorite insights found in these pages is learning how to "let God love you through, and in, the mess," as Kathryn puts it. When you've got six children at home, "mess" is a concept you are familiar with—even if you're a type A super-organizer who has color-coded bins for each child's Legos. This holy mom humbly admits that no solvent or shelving unit will take care of cleaning her spiritual house. She knows that it's when we allow God to do what is his very essence: to love us, and love us *big*. Then it's our turn.

But loving "big" in a holy family doesn't have to mean expense or extravagance. In Kathryn's Instagram story for Valentine's Day, 2019, she says, "Y'all, love is always in the little things. Love is most often found in doing the things that people don't see. There are a million ways to show someone you love them and it always involves sacrifice." I'm pretty sure it was Jesus who demonstrated that "loving big" means sacrificing our lives for others. And sacrifice, it seems to me, is the key ingredient to a holy family.

Now, just in case you don't have a family of eight and are starting to think this is not the book for you, let me just say this: I'm a fifty-something celibate Catholic priest with no wife or children; yet while reading this book I teared up, laughed, cheered, prayed, took notes, was convicted of changes I need to make in my own life, and even put the book down to immediately write to a friend.

The opening prayer for Catholic Mass on the Feast of the Holy Family has us imploring God: "graciously grant that we may imitate them [Jesus, Mary, and Joseph] in practicing the virtues of family life and in the bonds of charity, and so, in the joy of your house, delight one day in eternal rewards." My prayer for you as you read *Live Big, Love Bigger* is that you may be inspired by the Whitaker family in practicing the virtues of family life and in the bonds of charity and that you too may delight one day in the eternal reward of heaven.

Blessings!

Fr. Dave Dwyer, C.S.P.
Executive director of Busted Halo Ministries
February 26, 2019

To be unknown to God is entirely too much privacy.

★ *Thomas Merton*

SUCKER PUNCHED BY GOD

I have a bad habit of opening my mouth when I should probably zip it. Maybe you do too?

Part of it is passion, at least that's what I tell myself. "Go big or go home" has been my motto for as long as I can remember.

For years, ALL CAPS Kathryn always had something to say. I believed the things I shared were just extensions of the life I painstakingly crafted to keep the world from seeing who I really am, what all my fears really are, and how I really love.

An intense worry of being "found out" by my closest friends drove me to build a perfect life, brick by brick, complete with a picket fence, a spotless mini-van, Pottery Barn decor, and kids clothed in Janie and Jack. I guarded who I really was pretty tightly. I was convinced that if any balls dropped, it would be my fault. Plus, not having the answers was an out-of-body experience I wasn't prepared to handle.

Have you ever felt that fear? (Please say yes.) The fear that if you show God—and the rest of the world— who you really are, you'll be standing on an island all by yourself? I had a pretty good gig going as the mom of four, with one on the way.

But God has a wicked sense of humor.

In 2009, we welcomed our fifth child, a premature baby, Luke. He was a dainty three pounds and change, and at nine days old, he was fighting for his life. Luke's chances of surviving were a stark two in ten.

In one fell swoop, that perfect house I handcrafted didn't just crumble; it crashed to the ground—glass shattered, walls caved in, pipes burst, and beams broke.

Granted, it wasn't the first time my faith life endured a sucker punch. But with each of the previous challenges I had been able to weather the storm, rally all my inner forces, and manage to get the perfect house back in order. There had never been anything a little spackle, paint, and strategically placed art couldn't hide.

But that was not the case this time. No amount of redecoration could hide or heal that massive hit to the heart and soul.

I was forced to look deep into the crevices of my life and realize just how much control I did not have. I was reminded of just how messy life can be—how messy life really is. But through the circumstances of Luke's birth and the effect it had on my other children and my marriage, I also found beauty and a deeper connection with a God who loves the *real* me and takes every trial and error and uses them for good.

That love awakened a desire to cultivate a life framed by intention. Instead of worrying about how clean the van was (who am I kidding, I still care about that), how put together the house looked, or where we vacationed, I started to take stock of the real person residing within my soul. What's the condition of *my* house? Is it centered on a desire to ask God to frame it with purpose? Or am I still trying to be the chief super-intendent and project manager?

The truth is I was a control freak who cared way too much about how things looked and not enough about how they really were. I could not detach myself from managing my own life. Truthfully, I didn't really want to.

"Hope deprives us of everything that is not God, in order that all things may serve their true purpose as means to bring us to God," says Thomas Merton, a Trappist monk and author of *No Man Is an Island*. "Hope is proportionate to detachment."

Hope is proportionate to detachment.

Luke—the child that I clung to the tightest, the baby I begged God to spare—was God's invitation to detachment. When I was with him at his hospital bed-side, all my worldly cares faded away. But as soon as I stepped foot out of the hospital, the cares came crashing in around me.

You and I have a lot of cares in our lives. I care about how tight my jeans are, how my hair looks, and what other people wear. I care what people think about me. I care how many followers I have on social media (did someone just unfriend me?!) and where other people are vacationing. I care if shoes are left in the hallway, if dishes are put away, or if my kids are making their beds.

Some of the cares we have are valid, but most are not.

There is something so tender and vulnerable about living a broken life. When your soul is exposed and all you want to do is climb out of the nightmare, you do not have time to pretend. You can't manage other people's emotions or worry about relationships. You have no bandwidth left.

In those dark, wee hours of the morning at Luke's neonatal intensive care unit (NICU) bedside, listening to the incessant beeping on the monitor and feeling the steady breath of my son whisper across my cheek, I found a God who was begging me to wake the hell up and be intentional. I mean, right after I threw a fit and told him he was completely and totally bananas. This God had been waiting for me to be purposeful and open to the life he had planned for me. And it looked absolutely nothing like that Pottery Barn–furnished house.

God knows how to find us in the darkness. As the rocking chair tick-tocked back and forth, with my son in my arms and the heart monitor slowly beeping his heart rhythm, we found our radio frequency. Trust me: I begged God to lighten the load. I cried so many tears fighting his plan, telling him I wasn't strong enough to be this child's advocate, heal my struggling marriage, and be a kind and generous friend or the mom my kids needed. I tried convincing him that he was wrong. He wasn't buying what I was selling.

So here I sit, a decade later, with a new, more intentional life. The darkness gave way to light. The fear led to detachment. The vulnerability paved a pathway to purpose, and we finally found our freedom—a freedom to love, to change, to seek adventure, to let things go, and to live a life truly centered on Christ.

As much as I wish I could outline a whole, fancy ten-item checklist for how to live a more purpose-filled life, it's impossible. Life isn't one long, laminated to-do list (even though my grocery list certainly is). Intention doesn't come in check boxes. The lessons our family learned transformed us in every way. For one, we got to enjoy copious amounts of excellent BBQ. But we also learned how to look at every area of our life, hand it to God, and say, "Redeem it." When I invite you to take a leap of faith in transforming your own life, bit by bit, know that I understand just how scary it can be. But do it anyway, y'all.

When we learn that a friend is diagnosed with a debilitating illness or suffering an intolerable season of life, we recognize the difficulty of the journey. We see her suffering and we often provide her with the space she needs. We find a way to forgive her inability to be all things to all people. We often excuse her from having to do all the things and be at all the places. But when *we're* the ones suffering, the ones struggling, the ones trying to catch our breath, we try to power through it all on our own. Surely *we* don't need the same space, the same kind heart, or the same understanding tribe of friends. Or do we?

Ultimately, you have to face the mirror and get honest about what God desires for your family, or you might as well hand the keys of your soul over to your calendar.

The question I couldn't avoid after Luke's birth was, *Is it worth it?* Your family culture, the relationships with the people you love most, your time, your body, your family vacations, your friendships, and your peace—are they worth it? At 2:00 a.m. when you're finishing up the volunteer project you said would be no problem, is it worth it? The thousands of dollars you spend on extracurriculars, the debt you accumulate buying a life you can't afford, is that worth it? Are you happy you said yes, or are you begging God for a reason to say no? Maybe it's time to start dividing things into two categories: a no or a *hell yes*.

Our family isn't perfect—have a seat at my dinner table and don't mind the spilled milk. But we are better. It has been a messy path to get this far, and I suspect it will always be that way. But I've learned this: when you let the littlest thing transform you, when you let God into all the places—and I mean *all the places*—you will be healed in ways you didn't even know you needed to be healed.

God's grace and mercy will simultaneously blindside you and fill you with gratitude. Because instead of chasing the life you think you deserve, you'll be basking in the freedom of intentional living. You'll stop trying to overdo life, and you'll start living it with a genuine heart—with love, with passion, and with purpose. That's what happens when you understand that being an imperfect disciple making imperfect choices with an imperfect heart for an all-loving and perfect God is living a *hell yes* kind of life.

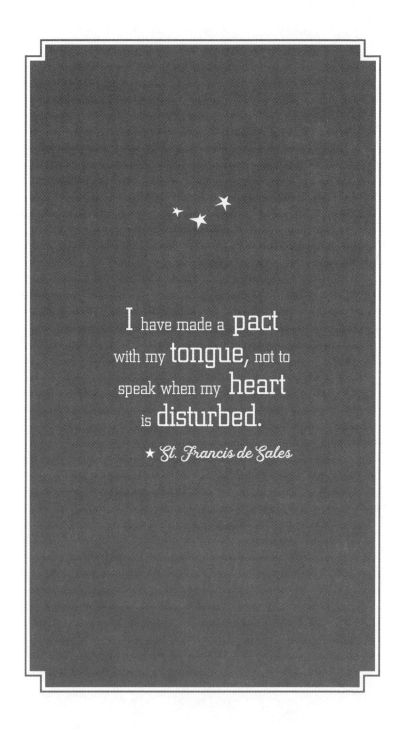

I have made a pact with my **tongue**, not to speak when my **heart** is disturbed.

★ *St. Francis de Sales*

Chapter 1

TALL DRINK
OF WATER

It was probably the best blind date I ever had. It surely beat the first one: that guy met me in a station wagon, filled with boxes of balloons for his vending job, and took me to Luby's, instructing me to order the LuAnn platter because it was cheaper. That's a true story, folks.

My blind date with Scott, however, was one for the history books. He met me on the quadrangle at Texas A&M University where the ROTC cadets lived with no balloons in sight. He was in a military uniform looking mighty handsome with his big blue eyes and his biceps, courtesy of a million pushups. A tall drink of water if I ever saw one. I wore a wrap skirt with fringe and cowboy boots with a giant sorority bow in my 1992 permed hair because I was BRINGING MY A GAME. Our lunch date was hardly quiet and quaint. Instead, we dined with two thousand other cadets in the dining hall. A few of Scott's outfit buddies joined us, along with the ranking captain and his two-year-old son, Larkin. It turned out to be one really loud, really big, group date.

Even though the conversation with Scott was occasionally interrupted with questions from the adorable tow-headed two-year-old sitting across from me, we both just smiled and kept eating. Scott's blue eyes and immaculate uniform kept my gaze, but his patience with Larkin captured my heart. He even skillfully sidestepped all the jeers from his buddies about the "cute date" he had. I was hooked.

We dated on and off, mostly on, for three years. I scored some awesome football tickets, trackside, during his yell leader days (that's Texas A&M speak for cheerleaders), and he accumulated an impressive Chi Omega sorority T-shirt collection. New Year's Eve 1995 he proposed at Reunion Arena in Dallas, where our serious dating had become official at a George Strait concert, three years prior. After my enthusiastic *yes*, we were well on our way to the picture-perfect, white-picket-fence life.

As Scott and I were preparing for marriage, Fr. Mike sat us down to discuss our FOCCUS (Facilitating Open Couple Communication, Understanding, and Study) premarriage inventory results. For the most part, the differences we had were negligible. Except one.

Fr. Mike shifted in his seat and smiled at both of us. "This statement, 'Children will change my life,' seemed to have polar opposite reactions."

I immediately was worried and Scott looked incredulous. I had answered "strongly agree" because how could you not? They would change everything!

Scott's "strongly disagree" was much more pragmatic: "I'm sure things will change, but it won't change the way I love you."

Fr. Mike smiled and winked. "Perhaps that's something that the two of you should discuss further as you prepare for marriage. Children can bring about drastic change in a marriage, but they also provide profound ways to grow in faith."

And with that, we let it lie.

After much preparation with Scott's hometown priest, I was confirmed an hour before our rehearsal dinner and became an official member of the Catholic Church.

Two weeks after the wedding, we started graduate school at Iowa State University and began our first year of marriage in Ames, Iowa. It was mostly good, with the occasional disagreement about artificial contraception and the introduction of babies. Our first argument was over my unwillingness to show Scott more physical affection because of my fear of getting pregnant on a practically nonexistent graduate student income. Our second argument was about whether our monthly budget could afford a once-a-week Coke from the vending machine—a whopping six dollars—during our weekly night seminar on agricultural leadership. Sex and money, that sounds about right.

As graduate students we were struggling to find a spiritual home in Ames. The collegiate church was a little too young for us, yet the other church was filled with a growing number of retired professors and only a few young families. However, after our first Mass at St. Cecilia, the Franciscan priest was eager to welcome us to the parish. He immediately recognized us as the "new kids," a perk of living in a small town. Fr. Terry encouraged us to come back the following week, and when we did, he had our parish registration papers ready along with the meeting date of a newly formed young marrieds group. He was sure we would fit right in.

A few weeks later, we sat in a room with four other young couples, three of whom had young children. I scarcely remember our discussion topic that evening, but I do remember after we prayed the concluding prayer, one of the couples said, "Hey, who wants to go out for beer and appetizers?" Those couples fed Scott and me with so much more than libations and great food though. These couples were just a few years down the marriage road, and we gleaned so much goodness from them. They taught us how to pray, how to have fun, how to parent with love, and how to live our faith. They were real, honest, and hilarious. Scott and I became immersed in parish life, serving in various ministries. Those couples showed us how serving the church can feed a marriage. Nearly two decades later, we still keep in touch with three of the four couples, and among us we have twenty-one children.

Two years later, we finished our master's degrees and began our first professional jobs in Indianapolis, Indiana, with the National FFA (formerly Future Farmers of America). As excited as we were about our careers, the same fears about finding the right church crept back in. We visited a few, but nothing really felt right. After procrastinating for too long one Sunday, we stumbled into the Sunday evening youth Mass at Our Lady of Mt. Carmel. We must've overlooked God's blinking neon sign over the church that evening that said, *This place will change your life*. The praise and worship music may have immediately spoken to my former-Protestant heart, but it was the energy bursting from those church walls that drew us in. We fell in love hard and fast for the youth program, our priests, and that community.

Prior to the Indiana move, we were living what I'd call a Christian-based life, but so many Church teachings really eluded us. Instead of trying to reconcile and understand them, we pushed them aside. The great thing about becoming volunteer youth ministers, though, is that teenagers don't ever let you off the hook. They, more than anyone we encountered at Our Lady, challenged us. We found ourselves asking the hard questions about some of the Church's biggest teachings and sacraments—artificial contraception, life, social justice, priestly celibacy, and confession. The answers took time and they didn't come easily, but the dialogue began because hormonal teenagers made us come face-to-face with our biggest questions of faith.

A year later, we were invited to go on pilgrimage as adult chaperones with the youth group. We had no idea just how it would change the trajectory of our marriage. We renewed our wedding vows in St. Peter's Square and even came back pregnant with our own Italian souvenir, our oldest son, Will. Some of the answers we had been searching for came a bit easier. It sure felt as if all the pieces of the faith puzzle were beginning to build a strong foundation for our marriage.

A second pilgrimage to Italy, a trip to World Youth Day and a chance meeting with Pope John Paul II, really deepened our understanding of how faith and life intersect. When we arrived home, a job opened up in Texas for Scott, and we found ourselves at a crossroads. Texas was home, but Indiana sure had become a close second. Our Indiana friends felt like family. Ultimately, though, we made the decision to move south. It's possible that the thought of never having to shovel snow or wear a huge parka to endure the Midwest's winters made the decision *slightly* easier. (You can take the girl out of Texas, y'all, but you can't take Texas out of the girl.)

After our move home, three more babies followed. When I announced my fifth pregnancy to Scott, we were both elated, even though it meant five children in the span of eight years. This birth would come a touch more than two years after baby number four. Our white-picket-fence life sure felt pretty fabulous. That confidence unraveled quickly at my twenty-week ultrasound, however, when we were given the news that this baby would, in all probability, not make it to viability outside the womb (marked at twenty-four weeks), much less to term.

That devastating ultrasound rattled my usually optimistic and steadfast faith. I came home that afternoon and quietly shut the door to our bedroom. I stood in front of our bathroom mirror, laid one hand on my belly, covered my eyes with the other, and sobbed silently so no one knew how much I was hurting. *How could my body fail me like this? How could something so good and pure hurt so much? What had I done wrong?* My head knew this circumstance wasn't tied to a poor choice I'd made, but my heart felt entirely different. Over the course of the next few months I would continue to beg God to let my love be enough to heal this baby.

Luke was born four weeks early at a dainty three pounds. His emergency birth and precarious forty-four-day NICU stay left my heart very fragile. In many ways, it mirrored the state of my marriage. With each passing day, the distance between Scott and me became greater. We were only communicating about logistics. I was at the hospital all day hearing about Luke's progress and setbacks while Scott was busy working so he could save time off in case there were more hospitalizations or complications. As it turned out, there were many.

Dr. Gary Chapman, author of *The Five Love Languages*, shares that most people have a primary love language—physical touch, acts of service, words of affirmation, quality time, or receiving gifts. When that language is "spoken," they feel most loved. Not surprisingly, many men cite physical touch as their primary language. It was most certainly Scott's. I, however, was the captain of quality time, craving time with my husband that simply did not exist. The stress of Luke's birth put our sex life on pause for months following his birth. I was terrified of getting pregnant again. As a couple, we were using Natural Family Planning (a natural way of spacing pregnancies, without artificial hormones or pills), but I turned my fear of getting pregnant and having to do this all over again into an excuse to abstain.

That, paired with Scott's love language of physical touch, went *really* well. We were fighting about everything. Bills were coming in, and we were drowning in five-figure debt. Our four-year-old was acting out at home. I had no idea what the third grader and kindergartener were doing in school as I gave up checking their nightly folders, and somewhere in the middle was our oblivious two-year-old. I even fell asleep during the third grader's parent-teacher conference.

I cried more in that first year after Luke's birth than the previous thirteen years of our marriage combined. Emotional, completely sleep deprived, and stressed, I felt as if no one understood the fear I carried.

The breaking point was Luke's traumatic third emergency surgery at four months. As I sat in that hospital room, I could feel the weight of my life unraveling. To the world of Facebook, it sure looked as if Scott and I were handling it so very well. We were posting smiling photos, I was updating my blog with real (but not too real) posts, and I put on a brave face for visitors. But the walls of room 303 at Dell Children's Medical Center knew better. A dear friend brought me lunch one afternoon during that hospital stay. As an adoptive parent of three special needs children, Angela could see past the curtain. She gave me the number of the kindest and gentlest Christian marriage counselor.

"Don't wait until it's too late, Kathryn."

I finally allowed myself to lean into the vulnerability and reach out for help. When I mentioned Angela's words to Scott that night at the hospital, he hung his head and whispered, "I think she's right."

Therapy is such a taboo subject. So many people benefit from it, yet few talk about its healing graces. In some circles it's considered unnecessary and a crutch for weak people. After all, many Christians believe retreats, prayer, and community provide enough resources for people to overcome their obstacles. Honestly, that's crap. You don't fight cancer without consulting an oncologist or extract your wisdom teeth with pliers from the toolbox in the garage. Why do we treat struggles in marriage, or in our lives, any differently?

Had it not been for the example of Scott's boss, Austin's bishop Gregory Aymond (now the Archbishop of New Orleans) and his commitment to regular therapy, I'm not sure we would've ever considered it. His example was likely the first step in saving our marriage—overcoming the stigma of needing help.

We walked into therapy believing our families of origin were very similar. We walked out understanding that while they were certainly full of a tremendous amount of support and love, every family has its struggles and challenges. One family tended to be passive-aggressive while the other relied on shame as a communication tool. We had brought both the good and the bad into our marriage, just like every other couple. The key was learning how to highlight the awesome and work through the struggles. I liken it to the kid who makes straight As in high school and then gets her backside handed to her in college because she doesn't know how to study (ahem, not that I learned that firsthand or anything). We had coasted through the first thirteen years of our marriage in the straight-A camp, but college courses with a steep learning curve really threw us. We had to decide if we were going to drop the class or meet with the professor and get a game plan. We humbled ourselves and sought help. It was crazy hard but necessary to begin healing.

Why couldn't my husband see that I couldn't speak his language of physical touch? Between pumping and holding a medically fragile child nearly twenty-four hours a day, I was touched out. I'd had enough. Our friends were showering us with help at home—kids at playdates, people mowing our yard and grocery shopping for us. Yet even with that assistance, I couldn't find the energy to tend to my own marriage.

Our therapist gave us reading homework, Dr. John Gottman's *The Seven Principles for Making Marriage Work*. Gottman and his researchers studied hundreds of marriages and discovered four predictors of divorce, also known as "the four horsemen": criticism, defensiveness, contempt, and stonewalling. It was a clean sweep; we exhibited all four. But just as the student learns to study smarter, surrounding herself with good study buddies and taking her assignments seriously, we approached healing our marriage in much the same way.

We were facing our biggest challenge as a couple—navigating more than a dozen specialists, surgeries, and therapy appointments for our son—but somehow we felt empowered. We were no longer passengers in our marriage, taking the curves in the road as they came. Instead, we were in the driver's seat, with the GPS on, guiding us to the best route.

We met with our marriage counselor once a week for nearly three months. Those weekly joint sessions gave us three concrete things that re-formed how we envisioned marriage: a safe space, a time for reconnection, and a purpose.

In her office, we gained a safe space to share what was really tearing us down. What used to be harmful and hateful words turned into someone walking us through the hate, to see the love and get to the core of our struggle. The wise words from Dr. Seuss, "hurt people hurt people," are so very true; we were living it. Now, when I see the venom emerge in myself, my spouse, or someone I love, I know there's always a root cause. That knowledge has changed my relationships in a real and lasting way.

Scott and I had gotten into a bad habit of simply becoming cohabiters in our home, merely exchanging logistics. By changing our afternoon routine to include a simple five-minute reconnection we were able to transform a tense period into one we look forward to every day. Scott walks in the door from work, and I immediately set aside whatever I'm doing. We hug, kiss (the kids *really* love that part), and decompress. It's long enough for him to feel appreciated through physical touch and me to be listened to by an adult, feeding my love language of quality time. We always reconnect for a longer period either in the late evening or early morning, but that five minutes gives us a crucial boost.

No organization, event, or human relationship can truly flourish unless it has purpose. But we're no Fortune 500 company, looking to maximize profits by restructuring our personnel. Instead, we're a partnership, with equal shares and lots of kid collateral. We had to spend time discerning what was most important to our family. *How did we want to spend our time? What made us the kind of family God desired us to be?* That only comes when you allow yourself to be vulnerable with the person you love—to share your innermost fears, dreams, and insecurities—so that they may encourage and strengthen you. It's a bit like a free fall for love. That became possible when we finally realized we were tethered to God and he would never abandon us, even in our darkest moment.

Authenticity in marriage is almost as hard to find as is true and abiding love in Hollywood. According to my Facebook feed, every couple jets to New York to enjoy a five-course dinner and see a show on Broadway, all while looking stunning in a tuxedo and a Rent the Runway dress. Hello, life with a serious filter.

When I was a kid, we used to go snow skiing and my mom would always holler after me as I zoomed down the mountain, "Ski with people who challenge you. It's the only way you'll improve!" The same thing applies to marriage. Seek out the people in your life with strong marriages to emulate instead of comparing yourself to the internet's highlight reel.

I don't know what problems challenge you or what brings you to your knees—addiction, infidelity, gambling, work or money problems, debilitating illness, abuse, disinterest, a special needs child, or something else. Let's be honest, no marriage is perfect, and no couple has arrived. I've seen, firsthand, how God can redeem even the most hopeless one.

Counseling taught us how to free-fall for Jesus and lean into the adventure he set before us. That free fall didn't happen overnight. It took time for Scott and me to trust, be vulnerable, and fall back in love again.

Nearly a decade after Luke's birth, we found ourselves in Europe celebrating our twentieth wedding anniversary (courtesy of a business trip and frequent flier miles). Our nine days in Europe were filled with lost bags, rain during a special anniversary photo shoot, a closed church, a missed bullfight, and an hour-long car rental line. But you know what else it was filled with?

Big love.

We shopped for toiletries in a Spanish plaza (I'm still not 100 percent sure if I bought hairspray or hair gel). Rome's skies blessed us with a magnificent rainbow at that photo shoot. That closed church gave us front-row seats to a fancy wedding send-off and an unexpected Marian procession in the streets of Seville. Missing the bullfight allowed us to enjoy tapas and beer with complete strangers at some hole-in-the-wall mercado in Madrid (*definitely* the better choice). And that excruciating car rental wait put us in Fatima just in time for Mass and a Rosary beneath the famed tree.

Yes, we went through hell and back as a couple, but we chose to put love first, seek help, and cast aside our fears. I don't know what the most important relationships in your life are like or the mountains you may have to climb with the people you love. But let me offer this: say yes to the blind date, put on your A game clothes, don your best cowboy boots, and hold tight to that tall drink of water. Love is worth it. I promise.

He made them, the
vicars of his love.

★ St. Ambrose

Chapter 2

SURPRISED BY THE COLLAR

★ ★ ★

In college, Scott and I spent way more time than was probably healthy at our favorite lunch spot, Freebirds. It's a divine burrito place, and any Texas Aggie will tell you it is far superior to its competitors. I've been getting the same order for the last twenty-five years—whole wheat tortilla, black beans, Spanish rice, Monterey jack cheese, white chicken, BBQ sauce—and maybe guacamole, if I'm feeling like the $1.40 splurge. One afternoon, Scott and I were deep in conversation. About halfway through our burritos, an unusual sight caught my eye.

The local priest assigned to St. Mary's, the campus parish at Texas A&M, had just walked in the door. Fr. Mike and a group of students were quite gregarious, laughing and high-fiving while they waited to order.

My eyes widened. It took Scott a few more bites before he realized I wasn't eating. "What's wrong, Kathryn?" I locked eyes with him, lowered my voice and whispered, "They let him leave the church?" raising my eyebrow for added emphasis. Scott nearly fell out of his chair laughing.

"Of course they let him out of the church," Scott chuckled. "He's a priest, Kathryn. He goes everywhere you and I do!"

Let's just add that misconception to the long list of myths I believed about the Catholic Church. Growing up Protestant in a small Texas Panhandle town with friends ranging from Baptist to Methodist, Unitarian to Pentecostal, and Episcopalian to Jewish, I was nothing if not ecumenical. I had plenty of opportunities to be surrounded by a multitude of good and holy pastors from various denominations. Of course, they were all married and had children, so they mirrored what I knew in my own home. Celibate priests and religious sisters were a bit of a foreign concept, existing only on my television.

Seeing Fr. Mike out and about was only the second time I had been in the presence of a priest; the other time was at a Catholic wedding. I certainly never saw any priests at events, at the grocery store, or dining out in my small town. To see Fr. Mike enjoying a meal outside of the hallowed walls of a church, laughing and conversing with college students, really caught me off guard.

Each encounter with all those ministers from my youth deepened my appreciation for those who chose to serve the church—no matter the denomination. The worship services were practiced differently, but I could clearly see they were aimed at the same Jesus. Becoming Catholic shifted my paradigm because I expected every priest to be monochromatic, with similar charisms (gifts given by the Holy Spirit that benefit the Church) because they all wore the same collar and belonged to the same Church.

I often reflect back on that lunch partly because of how absurd it was for me to believe that priests never left the church. It was a pleasant surprise to know that a priest's love of God went beyond preaching from the pulpit, anointing the sick, and conferring other sacraments—they actually leave the church, for one! Each priest carries his own set of gifts and talents, and each one we have known has served our family in unique ways. They have continued to show up in our life, rarely where or when I expected them and almost always with a profound gift of presence, wisdom, community, and comfort.

Just after Scott and I married and started to feel settled in our new parish community, I started looking for ways to get involved. When Fr. Terry found out I was a convert to the faith, he winked and said, "I know just the ministry for you." He pointed toward the Lectionary sitting at the front of the church, the large book that we use at Mass for the scripture readings. He knew I had a deep and lasting love of the Bible and proclaiming the Word at Mass as a reader was a perfect fit. He knew, long before I did, how God wanted to use me to serve others.

Before our children arrived, we were acquainted with a handful of priests because of my husband's career as a fundraiser for the Catholic Church. Fr. Kevin was instrumental in the early years of our marriage, helping us to find a way to strengthen our faith. He oversaw the youth ministry program at our Indiana parish. I had never seen a priest interact with youth as he did—he was engaged and relatable, and he challenged them to be their best selves. Nothing gets you thinking about your faith quite like teenagers and their endless questions.

Somehow, Fr. Kevin convinced us to walk a million miles with those teenagers on two Italian pilgrimages. During one of them, we had the providential chance to attend the canonization (when the pope officially declares someone a recognized saint of the Catholic Church) of St. Pio of Pietrelcina, an Italian priest. We learned of his canonization date a few months before our group departed, and Fr. Kevin rearranged our travel schedule so we could attend. Before you get all starry-eyed about how amazing it must be to stand in St. Peter's Square for the declaration of a modern-day saint (St. Pio died in 1968), let me break it down for you: half a million people, one-hundred-plus degrees, no wind, *hours* of sitting in the blazing June sun, long lines for the bathrooms in St. Peter's Square, and no shade. People were fainting left and right, and I was absolutely miserable. My canonization is clearly next (cough, cough).

During the metro ride back to our bus following the Mass, one of the adult chaperones looked at me and said with a kind smile, "Someday, Kathryn, you're going to look back on this day and be grateful you were here." On June 16, 2002, I couldn't see the lasting effect this priest had on thousands. Today, it is a different story.

My friend Lynne was right—I am more than grateful. I came home and dove into the book *Padre Pio: Man of Hope* and was taken aback at how deeply he loved God and how passionately the devil pursued him. St. Pio was known to sit in the confessional for hours, barely pausing to rest before starting it all over again the next day. In a culture that shies away from radically loving anything except our own selfies on Instagram, his faith example challenges me to be intentional and generous with my heart.

Fr. Richard, another parish priest in Indiana, and I bonded over two unlikely things—a love of the liturgy and sarcasm. He often facilitates a slow-motion Mass, where he celebrates the service, pausing to explain just how and why we celebrate the liturgy the way we do. As a convert, I found it fascinating. The importance Fr. Richard put on celebrating Mass with great care and deep faith planted the seed in me—the desire to find peace in the routine of the liturgy. He also taught me to lighten up and find humor and perspective in life. God bless the pastor who has a sense of humor. When a job offer gave us the opportunity to move back to Texas, it was met with some trepidation as our five years in Indiana had been especially transformational. Upon hearing the news, Fr. Richard responded, "God came to comfort the afflicted and to afflict the comfortable, *and you people are too comfortable!*" Basically, "Get your butts back to the Lone Star state; you have work to do." Classic Fr. Richard.

Our interactions and genuine friendships with Fr. Kevin and Fr. Richard gave us a solid example of how to minister to others, right where they were. Because of them, I fully understood the importance of showing

my children how to have healthy, loving, and respect-
ful relationships with the people who guide their faith
lives.

Not all of our interactions with priests have been
so full of love and joy, though.

When I first met Fr. Phil during our marriage
preparation, he was affable and welcoming, especially
once he learned I was interested in joining the Catholic
Church. He was able to minimize the formal process so
I could be confirmed prior to our wedding, six months
later. A priest Scott grew up with, Fr. Phil was a major
reason I decided to convert to Catholicism.

Nearly a decade after we married and shortly after
we moved back to Texas, we received devastating news.
In addition to a money embezzling conviction, Fr. Phil
was accused of inappropriate interaction with minors.
He was removed from ministry and died a few years
later, just before he was stripped of all priestly duties.

We were left reeling. Not only had this priest celebrated the Sacrament of Matrimony for us but he had
traveled to Indiana to baptize our oldest son and slept
in our home, holding Will in his arms each morning
while I cooked breakfast. I was horrified to think that
a priest and a man we dearly loved was capable of
such evil. Reconciling ourselves with this new truth
felt impossible. I deeply mourned the loss of the man
whom I had held in such high regard. Coming to terms
with that betrayal of trust and its deep wounds took
time and a heavy dose of mercy. It's the reason I pray
fervently for good and holy priests and why my heart
is especially tender as I seek to find faithful men to spiritually guide me and my family.

I stayed away from the confessional for a long time after learning the news about Fr. Phil. I found it difficult, at best, to trust priests with the most intimate details of my faith, and my prayer life was suffering. A few months after I gave birth to our third child, our parish was offering a penance service during Advent. My heart was focused on tending to a new life, and I felt myself being called back to the sacrament.

With three kids ages five and under, I decided to attend and was relieved to see a familiar face in Fr. David, a coworker of my husband's and a beloved priest to our family. He invited me and all three of the kids into the confessional room. The kids were old enough to (mostly) behave themselves but young enough not to repeat my sins to the greater Austin area.

Confession began easily as I rattled off the usual— lack of patience, gossip about others, and gluttony in partaking of way too much Dr Pepper and chocolate. As I shared the weight of the easy-to-confess sins, transitioning to the greater burdens on my heart, particularly my inability to have a regular prayer life, Fr. David kindly interrupted me. "Kathryn, you have to quit praying like a nun and start praying like a mom." He was the second of twelve children and the son of a labor and delivery nurse. Fr. David knew a thing or two about family life.

My first reaction was, *Did a priest just tell me that I was praying wrong?!*

I was feeling like a failure—as a mom, a wife, a friend, and a Christian. But Fr. David's words gave me the freedom to quit lamenting over all those failures and embrace the current season of my life. Instead of obsessing over five minutes of uninterrupted prayer

time or where to set up a prayer corner in our house, he
gave me permission to sneak in prayers of thanksgiving
while I washed dishes, did the laundry, or swept up
Cheerios. I had the freedom to use carpool as an opportunity to blast praise and worship music (or George
Strait depending upon my mood) and whisper Hail
Marys under my breath to prevent me from putting my
handmade artisanal kids up for sale on Etsy. When the
kids started arguing, they could recite the Our Father in
between hip checks and shoulder jabs. As a family we
could recite nightly prayers amid the screaming, full-
body contact and near constant interruption because
that's life.

I had been waiting for a block of designated quiet
time instead of fully embracing Jesus in the chaos.

We started keeping the Christmas cards we received
each year, pulling a couple from the pile each evening
at the dinner table to pray for those families. We looked
for ways to serve our community as a family—things
such as planting gardens at the Community First! Village homeless community, making dog toys out of old
T-shirts, and wrapping Christmas presents for children
in need.

Instead of stressing out about where I would find
time for God, I asked him to find it for me. Every day,
he looks at my planner and finds a way to open my eyes
to his abundant love. Sometimes, it's in the drive-thru
lane at Chick-Fil-A (my pleasure, I can hear God say)
or watching one of my kids serve a sibling. It is almost
always smack dab in the crazy of family life.

I was trying to be an overachiever (again!), and
a priest reminded me to be present in the smallest of
ways. He gently nudged me toward a love of my own

station in life instead of trying to embrace someone else's. It was transformational. That priest is now a bishop and the godfather to my oldest daughter. He is a wise man of God, who also happens to be a master woodworker and storyteller.

When Luke entered the world, our relationships with other people drastically changed, especially with priests. Before, they had been sources of laughter, levity, and great wisdom, but now their faith was our buoy in a life that felt as if it was spinning out of control. Luke's interrupted heartbeat while in the NICU permanently shifted my outlook on grace. As we were praying with a priest in my hospital room, Luke coded and had to be resuscitated. Less than half an hour later his godfather, Fr. Dean, arrived in the NICU, and the first thing he performed was an emergency Baptism.

It was these words from a priest—*I baptize you, Luke, in the name of the Father and of the Son and of the Holy Spirit*—that paused the chaos. The room fell silent (a rarity in the NICU), and all I could feel was the sanctity of the moment. For me, that instance radically changed our time in the hospital. I felt the instantaneous shift in who I was and who God desired for me to be. It didn't mean that God didn't tick me off later or that I became eternally pious. But God gave me new eyes, new ears, and a new heart—all at the hands and words of a priest. The world has never looked the same since.

After numerous hospital stays and surgeries, priests became an even greater part of our family's life. And I knew just how we were going to make them feel like family in our home and shatter the myths I carried for years: food, of course. Jesus' first miracle was at a wedding feast; he dined at table with his disciples the night before his crucifixion. Encounter happens at your dinner table, and ours was no exception.

On a regular basis, we have what we lovingly refer to as "vocation affirmation dinners" at our home. Because, really, nothing affirms a priest's decision to serve the Lord (or appreciate the quiet rectory) more than a raucous house of six kids spilling milk, fighting, and screaming for seconds. Having priests over for dinner is a win-win situation. We expose them to the realities of family life, which they so desperately need to be acquainted with to minister to the flock. In turn, we are exposed to a person who has chosen to dedicate his life to the ministry of the Lord. That radical love needs witnesses, and I'm grateful my dinner table sees it often.

Our rules for having priests over are simple: (1) they get to choose the meal, and (2) they have to wear their collar or a Texas A&M shirt (their choice). We don't use special dishes, nor do we hide the cobwebs. I do, however, clean the toilets because I have three boys. Those priests see us as we are, and amazingly, some still come back for seconds.

On one such occasion, Scott's boss—the bishop—joined us for dinner. While I flitted about the house, obsessing over whether the Legos were picked up or the bathroom had pee stains around the toilet, the kids continued to be *kids*. On that particular evening, our house was so very full of energy, aka "normal." As we put the last kid to bed, Bishop Aymond quietly sat down on our couch, with a glass of wine in hand, and grinned. I braced myself for the comments of "Oh, your hands are full" or "Aren't they full of energy?" But you know what he said?

"I feel so at home here."

With that simple statement he became my new favorite dinner guest. As someone who loves to have people over to the house, that's always forefront in my mind: Will they feel as if they belong here?

Making people feel at home with us, especially when we celebrate sacraments, is my primary goal. I mean, it isn't *really* a party at our house until there's a priest hearing confessions in the front yard while my kids fight over whose turn it is in cornhole. Fr. Tom, one child's godfather and another's confirmation sponsor, is a treasured member of our family. He served his pastoral year of seminary—like student teaching for priests—at our parish and spent a fair amount of time at our house playing Jenga and watching Aggie football. In his former life, he was a police officer, so his interrogation skills are on point. More than any other priest, Fr. Tom pushes me to be fully honest with myself and with God, asking me the questions that need pondering and prayer. There is no pretending around him.

It's easy to invite priests over for the good and joyful. We've invited them over to bless our new home, watch NFL playoff games while eating all our queso and drinking sweet tea (looking at you, Fr. Dave), cheer on the Aggies, play Jenga, and celebrate sacraments. But it's important—and necessary—to invite them into the dark places where you sit in fear. It's where God does his most magnificent work.

Each time Luke was hospitalized post-NICU, we were housed at the same Catholic hospital, Dell Children's in Austin. The Catholic chaplain, Fr. Richard, would always show up in our room within an hour of our admission. I started to wonder if he had a GPS tracker on us. Turns out he was in the habit of checking the hospital census each morning, looking for names he recognized. The hours he spent with us—hearing our confessions, administering communion, or giving us tips on which hospital food to avoid—were clutch. In the hospital when the stakes are high, there is rarely pretense. With Fr. Richard, we were able to set aside the facade that everything was OK. He knew better. He just kept meeting us where we were. As horrible as it was to be a resident at the hospital, I knew he and Jesus would meet us there.

Indeed, I have been nurtured and encouraged by a multitude of spiritual fathers. They have helped me parent with intention, love the liturgy, appreciate humor, hold fast to my faith, enjoy really good queso, build community with purpose, cheer on the Aggies, ask the hard questions, and change for the better.

I don't know what's troubling your heart or what has you in desperate prayer, but I know that when you stop trying to be the strongest one in the room, you may just be surprised by the beauty and wisdom of the collar and the man who wears it.

We no longer see internet tools as products released by for-profit companies, funded by investors hoping to make a return, and run by twentysomethings who are often making things up as they go along. We're instead quick to idolize these digital doodads as a signifier of progress and a harbinger of a new world.

★ Cal Newport, DEEP WORK

Chapter 3

#FREAKOUT

(As you read this chapter, please don't think about how badly this dates me. Love, an Atari fan for life.)

Raise your hand if you remember sitting in computer class with a glass monitor as big as a refrigerator box, complete with a black screen and a blinking green cursor. Or better yet, who remembers typing class and fighting classmates for the one with the self-correcting tape already installed?

As coeditor of my high school yearbook, we used to take photos with film and then develop them in the darkroom. Our layout pages were all hand-drawn, and we sent in hard copies of our ideas to the publisher. My senior year, we were just starting to type feature stories and lead articles on computers—so we could print them out.

When I went off to college, I carried a three-ring notebook, a stack of notecards, and a fistful of pens. Nobody even had a computer, much less a laptop. Email was starting to gain popularity my senior year of college. To complete my graduate school thesis research, I had to make a six-hour drive (one way) from Ames, Iowa, to Champagne, Illinois, so I could access the microfiche files of old magazine issues of *The Progressive Farmer*, *Modern Farmer*, and *Farmers Weekly*. Thankfully, I had a friend in law school there to give me access to the library and who let Scott and me spend the night so we could make the six-hour drive back the following day.

That's laughable now.

At my first job, we were launching the website for the National FFA Organization and still using dial-up internet connections. Cell phones came in zipper bags, and "social media" wasn't even a phrase. Shoot, we were using calling cards to make long-distance phone calls!

In my early years of motherhood, there were no Facebook groups or Instagram direct messages where I could reach out to other moms in the trenches. Nope. I had to haul my happy butt up to the church and sit in a meeting with other moms to get answers to all my burning questions or schedule a playdate with a friend. My mom would probably remind me that groups like *that* didn't exist when she was a young mother. You either asked your own mother or figured it out by reading books written by people like Dr. Spock. My first pediatrician even hosted "morning call hour" where parents could call his home number from 7:00 to 8:00 a.m. and ask him any question, all while he drank his morning coffee and ate his whole-wheat toast. We've come a long way from all that. Now we can order strep tests via Amazon Prime and have a doctor prescribe antibiotics via an app on our phones.

Having a big and wide family has allowed me to see the influence of digital technology on my mother-hood journey. With baby number one, I nursed Will to sleep praying Hail Marys, using my fingers as beads. When I needed to get my husband's attention in the other room, I whispered just loud enough for the audio monitor to pick up my pleas for help. And the look of my baby's sweet, content face was captured simply in my memory. By the time baby six rolled around, I could listen to the Hail Marys being recited on the Spotify app on my smartphone, text my husband for help, send a video of Gianna sleeping to family, or buy something on Amazon Prime I'd just seen while scrolling through Instagram. Progress, or distraction?

I'm not a digital native, but I'm raising six of them, and I count it as my highest hurdle as a parent and as a woman.

Preliminary studies exist, but no one knows the real long-lasting effects of what it means to *be* a digital native or to *raise* one. For that, I've come to learn, our family relies on three things: healthy boundaries, a moral compass, and a supportive community.

One evening, while closing out all the windows on the kids' computer, something prompted me to look in the internet's browser history. A string of porn sites lit up the screen. I was in disbelief, then denial. Statistics tell us that a staggering amount of teenage boys and girls are exposed to pornography before age eighteen.

With such easy access, it's not a matter of *if* your kids see porn, mom and dad, it's *when*.

I'm no stranger to addiction. As the granddaughter of an alcoholic, I saw the ugliness of dependence and the struggle of an enabler. I thought my grandmother's alcohol addiction taught me how to spot someone struggling, yet porn entered our home right under my watchful eyes. We were working to cultivate a home rich in goodness, right judgment, love, and holy purpose, and my "accidental stumble" onto the browser's history reminded me to be on guard and fight evil with some holy assistance.

Maybe you feel as I do, that the fight for our children's souls is overwhelming. It helps to remember that I am not responsible for all children of the world, just the six living under my roof. When Scott and I put concentrated and purposeful emphasis on being their teachers and role models, we protect their minds and prepare their character. The free will is all theirs. It's also why my knees are raw. Howdy, increased prayer life! We are learning to parent with grace in this digital age, avoiding shame and leading with love by establishing healthy boundaries. And they're healthy boundaries not just for our kids but for us as well.

When I got caught standing in the kitchen scrolling Instagram when I should've been cooking dinner, one of my children yelled, "You care more about your online friends than your real-life kids." Ouch. He wasn't wrong in that moment. As an effort to escape the hardness of the day, I had buried myself in my social media feeds, encouraging other people and lifting them up. Yet I was neglecting the needs of my own family just feet away from me. I felt so validated and important online, but in real life what emphasis was I placing on God? Those words stung, but for once I had no response. It was time to find balance.

Some of you may find that balance comes in a complete social media blackout. For others it comes in online monitoring apps, dedicated time for social media use, or deleting social media from a smartphone so it can only be accessed via a laptop. I don't know what your balance looks like, but I do know where it starts—on your knees, in prayer. FOMO (fear of missing out) is real. But if I'm missing out on my own life, built right in front of me, what kind of disciple am I modeling for my children?

When one of our kids downloaded the one social media app we forbid (it's always *that* one, am I right?), I reacted, badly. Maybe it's because the baby had just launched my cell phone off the two-story balcony in our living room. Thankfully, the baby, the teenager, and my cell phone all survived the cacophony. Barely. Calmer heads prevailed, we talked it through and set some boundaries for what was and was not acceptable in our household.

Of all my children, Will has taught us the most about "viral parenting." As the oldest, he is the first to experience everything, including our ineptitude as rookie parents in the digital world. There have been many late nights when he's taught us more about patience, courage, and understanding than we taught him.

For us, the sweet spot has been no cell phones until high school and no social media until at least age thirteen (and in some cases, older than that). There are some days I wonder if they're working on a world record for complaining about that approach. I keep reminding them that with freedom comes responsibility. Rather than parent out of fear—*but everybody is doing it, Mom, and I'm the only one not allowed*—we decided to parent with firm love, standing by our decisions. It's rarely popular and harder than hell, but we do it anyway.

The beauty, and the frustration, of parenting digital natives is that everything is new and it just keeps changing. Stop sending out updates, Instagram and Snapchat! We're all swimming without boundaries, searching for them as we go. But prudence never goes out of style. To set those boundaries, it helped when we defined our moral compass, sought out community, committed it to prayer, and then acted.

The moral compass gets a hip check almost every day. There are the two extreme camps. One says no digital devices and no social media until college because it's a pathway to a lost and distorted life. The other says give ten-year-olds (or even younger) the latest iPhone with no restrictions because they're going to be socially ostracized if they don't have it.

Most of us, though, fall somewhere along the middle ground of that spectrum. We see and hear the reports of a cell-phone-addicted lifestyle; we feel the societal pressure, and we desperately want to help our kids manage it—even though we struggle with it as adults. Sometimes, though, I feel like the junkie, doling out illegal substances—both to myself and my teenagers—and then asking them to self-regulate.

It's like eating fast food. We know the calorie count and the hit to the wallet is real, yet we do it anyway because, dang, those Chick-Fil-A fries are good. The parallel between our sanity and cell phones is much the

same. Studies confirm what our hearts already know—
too much consumption of a digital world spurs depression, anxiety, isolation, bullying, and suicidal thoughts.

As avid social media users ourselves, Scott and I
want our children to fully appreciate the challenges
and joys of using it, while keeping the focus on making
real-life connections with people. The digital age crux?
Navigating the landscape with Jesus at our side. I won't
lie. It's a tightrope walk of faith. It's why I lean heavily
on cold beer and late-night text messages with a trusted
group of girlfriends, thick in the trenches with us.

When you build that community, do it knowing that your child will fall flat on his face and make
mistakes. In fact, I guarantee it. Extend grace to your
teenager (and to your friends) when the pitfalls come.
I say that with great passion because there have been
times during this digital parenting journey when I have
rushed right past grace and instead thrown some serious shame back at my child. It's ugly and humbling
when I do, but somehow, some way, God finds a way to
redeem it. It almost always starts with *please forgive me*.
The innocence of childhood and my inability to protect
it fully has been a hard pill to swallow. But just as we
did not survive those isolating days in the NICU alone,
we do not parent in a digital age alone either.

On Twitter one afternoon, I responded to a tweet
from Jennifer Fulwiler about the power of professional
counseling after a traumatic event. That led to a direct
message, a playdate, and a real-life friendship with a
Catholic mom I admired and respected. We also swore
we would never again plan a July playdate in Texas,
outside on a sweltering one-hundred-degree day. A
Facebook friend got me connected to a preemie mom

group in Austin. For several years we met on a monthly basis, sharing the woes of parenting medically fragile children and finding solidarity through it all. Instagram showed me pictorial proof my children weren't the only ones making bad choices. Somehow, we found the beauty in all of it, no filter required. Ironic that the same place that brings me so much anxiety in parenting also allays my fears and lifts me up on the hard days. The real challenge of parenting in the digital age, though, is maintaining a focus on real-life relationships. The digital world makes the initial introduction, and a real-life hug invites them inside.

Through blogging I discovered amazing women who were struggling just as much as I was. They were knee-deep in Mega Bloks and play food, craving a case of Dr Pepper and a hot bath too. Many of those internet friends became real-life ones. We *must* believe that the internet can redeem itself, because it *can*.

Luke's arrival brought about a significant shift in my view of community. As a self-proclaimed type A mom, I felt very much in control of my life and the lives of my children. That driver's seat sure felt good. The reality of our life, though, caused the illusion of control to disappear, and my eyes were opened. No parent has it fully figured out in every area. But when I shifted my thinking from competition to community, somehow the journey didn't feel quite as hard.

Providentially, I was connected to Hand to Hold, a nonprofit based in Austin for parents of premature infants. I have seen the good and beautiful of the internet and the absolute importance of real-life connections through their work. When I helped them launch a parent blog focusing on prematurity and the NICU, I found soul sisters in the trenches. We helped one another find pediatric specialists; we shared tips on the latest in feeding therapies and comprehensive care clinics. On the days when I cried to the internet through that preemie blog, there was a mom waiting to comment and lift me out of my despair, and it was so very life-giving.

I experienced the good of the digital new evangelization when it made it possible for me to physically reach out to another parent in need, sit at the hospital holding her hand, take her a meal, or just listen as she laid out all her fears. The digital age connects us; our hearts and hands make us real and genuine. If I can get my teenagers to put their phones down long enough, I know they'll experience it too.

The balance of an active digital presence to proclaim the gospel of Christ while making a concerted effort to be disconnected enough to be present to the people in our lives is one I struggle with every day. But I get up and try again every morning.

With parenting, filters don't exist. The kids see right through us. Things such as watching your own digital behavior, enrolling your kids in positive extracurricular activities that keep them engaged with real people, dutifully monitoring their online accounts, and praying over how to do it all will be your digital life song.

Make no apologies.

Don't let things such as porn and sexting fill you with fear and keep you from having the hard conversations with your children. Embrace how God wants to grow and stretch you by teaching your children to be powerful evangelizers in a digital world.

Have the conversations anyway. Someday—please Jesus—they will thank you, and you will praise God for his guidance and wisdom. Plus, you might even post that victory dance on Instagram.

In poverty as well as in
other misfortunes,
people suppose that friends
are their only refuge.

★ Aristotle

Chapter 4

CHICKEN WINGS, BEER, AND COLLEGE FOOTBALL

Growing up in a small Texas Panhandle town, there was a universal rule: everybody knows everybody else's business. My first warning for rolling through that stop sign? My mom knew before I arrived home because she saw the police officer at the grocery store and he delivered the juicy news. For most of us growing up in Dumas, we'd known one another since we were toddlers and lived just a short walk or bike ride away. Friendships were so easy at that age.

There were exclusive tree house clubs (meant solely for reading The Baby-Sitters Club books), slumber parties, neighborhood capture the flag, and free-range trampoline marathons. There was even the time I ran

away from home with a friend. Our suitcase was filled
with PB&J sandwiches and a dozen books. But after an
hour, we gave up because we were hot and needed a
bathroom. It was idyllic, really, until sixth grade, when
all my girlfriends got together, decided to call me "The
It," and convinced the entire class to ignore me all day.
The joke passed twenty-four hours later, and I was back
in the fray again. It was the first time I ever felt betrayed
by people I trusted; it stung for much longer than I'd
like to admit.

When I entered seventh grade and began junior
high, I was fitted for a back brace to correct my scoliosis and that stepped me into a whole new level of
awkward. But because four elementary schools fed into
that junior high, I met some new friends and began
to flourish. It figures that just as I was settling in, my
parents decided it was time to move to a bigger city for
my dad's new job. I hated my parents for about a year
and made darn sure they knew it. Tween girls are just
the most fun, aren't they?

As it turns out, Mom and Dad *did* know best. Moving to a new high school with people who knew nothing about me was a scenario that prepared me well for
so many other life transitions—when I went to college
nine hours from home, moved five states away for
graduate school, started a new job in a new state, and
then moved back to Texas again.

It was my high school friendship with Heather that
really showcased the beauty of a loyal friend. She was
a cheerleader, and I was a band nerd. She was popular
and kind; I was witty and awkward. But we both had
a healthy obsession with Dr Pepper and bonded over a
mutual disdain for our sophomore English teacher. I've

always wondered why Heather befriended the new girl, but the older I get, I know it is because her heart is pure and her love for Jesus so magnificent.

While life took us on different paths post-high school, we still remained close, writing letters and calling each other on a regular basis. When Scott and I were engaged, I enthusiastically asked Heather to be a bridesmaid in my wedding. A month before I married, though, I made a decision that should've fractured our friendship forever. I asked her to step out of my bridal party for reasons I look back on now and just want to bury my head in shame. I was prideful, judgmental, and ignorant. She had every reason to simply walk away. Heather should've sat me down, read me the riot act, and told me what a horrible person I was. Instead, she forgave me and welcomed me back into her life. It was one of the greatest acts of mercy God has ever bestowed on me. Heather saw me at my worst and loved me anyway.

Friendships—the kind that are true and lasting—involve sacrifice. They require you to forgive when you want to walk away, set aside your own agenda, carve out time in your busy day, put aside the to-do list, and just be. When you put your life in Jesus' hands, surrender your meticulously laid plans (trust me, my spreadsheet is long and well organized), and let him take the wheel, it's a magnificent step toward radical love.

In his book *Nicomachean Ethics*, Aristotle shares three distinct types of friendship: beneficial, pleasant, and excellent.

Raise your hand if you've been in a beneficial, or useful, friendship. It's not built on a firm foundation of trust or depth, and it tends to quickly fade away once a person no longer feels the friendship is benefitting her or her efforts.

For most of us, and in most seasons of life, I believe the bulk of our friendships reside in the pleasant category. We are relational people, so how a person makes us feel helps us decide to pursue a deeper relationship or be content with its current state. In a sense, I think we "date" our friends, testing the waters to see if they're someone we simply share common ground with or if they are a lifetime kind of gal. Pleasure friendships often occur because of a shared life experience or a geographic location; we work out together, we share the same alma mater, or we live in the same neighborhood. When we are around them, we experience joy, solidarity, and support. Yet we tend to hold back on the deeper, more precious memories because we aren't quite ready to share them.

Ironically, in an age in which we are virtually connected and can know the absurd minutia of hundreds, if not thousands, of people, we still feel isolated. It's because friendships of pleasure and utility are short-lived. They are temporal, changing due to personalities, activities, or geographic location.

Excellent friendships—the kind that we all yearn for because they promise unconditional acceptance and love—are much harder to find and cultivate. It *seems* easy, on paper, to find excellent friends. A quick scroll through Instagram's hashtags of #BFF, #bae, and #besties lulls us into the lie of ease. Friendships rooted in faith and virtue require work and commitment and sometimes giving up things we love. They force us to focus on the long game of contentment, not the short one of convenience. I am drawn to my excellent friends because they focus on the process of imitating God. The older I get, the smaller my faith tribe grows and I cultivate a deeper connection with the ones who remain.

It was through my isolating experience in the hospital with Luke that I begged God to send me an excellent friend who could fully appreciate the hardness of the season. And in the door—literally—walked Dina.

Kelli, my NICU mentor, introduced us in the doorway of Luke's hospital room at Dell Children's Medical Center. Dina's youngest son, Reece, was born a few weeks after Luke and had already endured the same number of surgeries. It didn't take us long to find commonality. When you're in the third ring of hospital hell, you long for someone who gets what it's like to be in your shoes. There is no explaining or apologizing; there is simply understanding.

Dina and I exchanged cell numbers, and a friendship was born. A month later, Luke was back in the hospital's pediatric intensive care unit (PICU) for a planned spinal surgery. Scott was at the house with the kids, and I was desperate for a shower. I think it had been three days since I'd had one. I sent a text to Dina, lamenting my sad state. Half an hour later, she appeared at the PICU door, with her arms held wide to hold Luke. I walked across the hall for a very glamorous and relaxing hospital shower, because nothing says, "I feel so refreshed" like hospital soap. We still laugh about that, and I remember how touched I was that someone knew how much I needed to feel the tangible love of a friend, even if I did smell like antiseptic cleaner.

Three weeks later, it was Dina and Reece's turn in the PICU, and the situation was dire. Her text message came in, and I was at the hospital just minutes later.

In my panic and worry, I grabbed one of our Italian rosaries, blessed by Pope John Paul II, to give to her. My experience told me nothing I said would matter; it was simply my presence and prayers she craved. She lovingly took that rosary and squeezed me tight. Reece came home, healed and healthy, less than a week later. When I shared with a mutual friend about my gift of the rosary, she gasped. "Kathryn, you know she's Jewish, right?"

Y'all, this scenario plays out in my life time and time again—I act before I think. This time, though, it turned out to be a delightful gift. When I went to apologize, Dina wouldn't have it. "That rosary is precious to me, Kathryn, because you gave it to me out of love, and that's all I needed." She and her family have helped us celebrate the Catholic sacraments of First Communion and Confirmation and we have been there for her boys' bar mitzvahs and her father's *shiva* (a traditional week of mourning after death). It has been a beautiful and mutual relationship of trust and love. Our boys share almost all the same specialists, and we are both NICU mama bears. We fear no billing office or insurance company, and neither of us is afraid to speak our mind with a specialist.

I trust Dina with my greatest fears, and she in turn provides a tremendous safety net of love. Together our NICU warriors have endured thirteen surgeries but only one shared hospital stay. What are the odds we would meet on that *one* stay, on the very last day? I like to call it a God-chance.

After Luke was born, I really struggled to find commonality with other women. The world felt heavier and harder, with medical bills mounting and specialist visits to attend to; I felt as if no one really understood my day-to-day life as a mom to a medically fragile child. I found myself withdrawing to my blog to sort it all out. If I couldn't find other women who understood, then maybe I could help another mom on the internet who was struggling too. That drive to help led me to serve as the lead blogger for Hand to Hold's parent blog. Through it, I found my confidence and my voice again.

For the first time since Luke's birth I felt empowered. The life that I had put on pause to care for him was starting to trickle back. It looked different though. It was more focused and intentional, and I became incredibly purposeful about finding excellent friendships to foster with other women. And that's when I found Susan.

Susan and I met online (and this is where it starts to sound like Stalkers R Us, but I swear this was legit) over a shared love of agriculture, cold beer, and our faith. That friendship grew deeper when she traveled to Austin with her newborn in tow for a women's conference and stayed at my house. We were fast friends. With thirteen kids between us, there was never a shortage of shared experiences. Our oldest boys were born just days apart, and we have navigated the sometimes-rocky, yet awesome, teenage years together with babies on our hips.

Nothing cements one of those excellent friendships faster than chicken wings, beer, and college football. I'm 100 percent certain of it. Susan's husband texted me to see if I was on board for an epic birthday surprise. Of course I was in—I'm the inventor of parties. This time, however, it was an intimate party of two. He had contemplated buying Susan jewelry, clothes, or a spa day, "but what she really wants is time with a friend," he told me.

Steve picked me up at the Wichita, Kansas, airport—it was the first time he and I had ever met—and we were both giddy with anticipation. When I followed Steve into the house that night, Susan was completely unsuspecting. She thought he was at the local high school football game with all the boys, while she nursed and stayed back with their youngest. I could see her exhaustion as she paced back and forth with a fussy baby. When she spotted Steve, the look of alarm was apparent. Why else would he be home unless something was amiss with the boys? Steve motioned to me. "Surprise!" we both yelled out. As I walked over to hug her, the four of us went down on our knees in tears.

Susan and I filled the weekend with middle school football, a beautiful lunch with her parents, a pedicure, and Mass. And yes, the wings, beer, and college football sure made it all worthwhile. All of that was beautiful and good, but it was the time we spent together—sharing the depths of our hearts—that made it a soul-filling kind of weekend. We always pick up where we left off, but we are never afraid to go deep, baring our fears, to one another. She and I have had some heavy crosses to bear (don't we all?), and our time together in person reminded me how much my heart thirsts for authentic friendship. In an age of social media likes and follows, many of us start to give way more than a damn about people on the internet than we do about the real-life people in front of us.

Like Pope Francis, I believe that social media can be a holy and worthwhile endeavor. In his message for the fiftieth World Communications Day in January 2016,

Pope Francis said it this way: "Emails, text messages, social networks and chats can also be fully human forms of communication. It is not technology which determines whether or not communication is authentic, but rather the human heart and our capacity to use wisely the means at our disposal."

I haven't figured out how to bi-locate between Kansas and Texas, so Susan and I rely on text messages, Instagram direct messages, the Voxer app, and the occasional FaceTime call to reconnect. She knows me in a way that few people do. I wonder, do you have someone like that in your life? Are you taking the time to look up from your phone and really connect with someone? Technology has kept the two of us in communication, but it has been crying sessions over a glass of sweet tea, ordering "as seen on TV" junk on the internet at midnight while laughing hysterically, and the knowing glances of understanding at Mass that have solidified our bond. Each time one of us departs, the tight embrace we share makes me feel how much I'm loved and how much I'm needed. I pray Susan feels the same.

I have been equally blessed with spiritual relationships with excellent friends I never thought I'd have: a whole gaggle of Dominican sisters. As a former Protestant, befriending a religious sister sure seemed a little farfetched. I think I simply believed I wasn't Christian enough (or they weren't allowed) to have friends among the laity. Remember, I was a Protestant who believed priests only lived at the church and never left the building!

However, when I was pregnant with my first child, Scott and I emceed an impressive youth retreat in Carmel, Indiana. At Destination Jesus, more than seven hundred youth, adult chaperones, keynote speakers, musicians, priests, and religious sisters and brothers were in attendance. It was there I met my very first Dominican (from the St. Cecilia congregation in Nashville), Sr. Anna Laura. She was spunky and faithful and had the best Arkansas accent—a welcome sound to my homesick southern heart. That friendship has remained for nearly eighteen years, and one of my daughters, Anna-Laura, is a daily reminder of the preciousness of that meeting and our lasting friendship.

Two orders of Dominicans we love, Nashville and Mary, Mother of the Eucharist ("Ann Arbor" as they're often known), both have a captivating presence. Ann Arbor Dominicans now teach my children in Catholic schools, and while the habit they wear is the same, the sisters are uniquely different. Some are studious, others athletic. Some sisters are boisterous while others are soft-spoken. The thing that has remained the same, however, is their unparalleled joy in their vocation. You can see it on their faces. They are in love with their spouse, Jesus, and all friendships they have flow from that love. It's remarkable, really, to be in their presence.

Just days before I gave birth to Luke, the Ann Arbor Dominicans arrived in our diocese to begin teaching in our Catholic schools. The first one I met was Sr. Maria Gemma. Maybe it was our shared love of Dr Pepper, but she and I were on the same wavelength almost immediately. In my darkest days of the NICU, she would always appear at the door or send me an email. That is not an exaggeration; it happened every time I cried out to Jesus to show me that he loved me and would not abandon our family. And it continues to happen to this day. She even has a running bet with my boys every Super Bowl game. The loser has to pray a Rosary for the winner, which really makes them both the winner, right?!

At many of the crucial moments in my life, there is the story of a sister attached to it. The day a beloved family member died, I headed straight for the convent and wept in their chapel. Sr. Maria Fatima and her fellow sisters laid their hands on me, and their steady voices prayed the Hail Marys of the Rosary as I succumbed to the overwhelming grief. The day the contract came in for this book, Sr. Maria Fatima was waiting with open arms to congratulate me in the school car line. I've often told her that I forgot she wore the habit. I relished our commonality long before I saw her veil. And when I decided to "replace" the Louisiana State University flag flying at the convent with one from Texas A&M, the hilarity that ensued in getting it back is still a great story. Just ask Sr. Elizabeth Ann. It's best told over margaritas and queso.

The hardest part of befriending sisters is knowing the order will likely send them to a new assignment in a year or two. I have to love them well while they're here in my presence. But Sr. Maria Gemma was quick to remind me she would see me at Mass, no matter where we both were. "See you at the Tabernacle," she always writes at the end of her emails.

Through my deep and abiding friendships with women such as Heather, Dina, Susan, and the sisters, I have witnessed some remarkable women who possess extraordinary faith. They are remarkable because they realize they are ordinary women, beloved by God, and they have a purpose to fulfill—to be excellent disciples.

The deepest, most satisfying friendships in life encompass all the emotions—the joy, the sorrow, the difficult, and the easy—because it's through those shared experiences through the hills and valleys of life, the love I have for them has been fortified. With each of those women, I decided not to move on to someone else because the friendship got hard. Rather, I decided to stay precisely because of it.

At every moment, we are volunteers.

★ Stephen Colbert

Chapter 5

CHECK
YOUR HEART

I grew up listening to country music legend George Strait. It's the hazard of being a sixth-generation Texan, growing up in the Panhandle where songs such as "Amarillo by Morning" are as popular with babies as "Jesus Loves Me."

George's songs, such as "Love Without End, Amen," got me through high school. He was with me straight through college, singing "I'm Carrying Your Love with Me" right into my first few years of marriage. My husband, Scott, even proposed to me using lines from George's very popular "Check Yes or No."

Maybe your George Strait is The Beatles, U2, Adele, Norah Jones, Matt Maher, or Neil Diamond (or maybe you think I need to get new musicians to love!). Whoever it is, when their song comes on the radio—your song—you are immediately face-to-face with a memory. Those songs have a way of not only transporting us back in time, even if for a moment, but also giving life to an experience we happen to be struggling with yet can't find the words.

My love of music helped me navigate my fear of death, which I avoided dealing with for the majority of my life. When my grandmothers died, there was no formal burial; it was simply a write- up in the obituaries and a small gathering of the family. One was cremated; the other donated her body to science at a local university. When my paternal grandfather died, I stayed home to study for middle school finals instead of joining the small family group that gathered at the cemetery to share favorite stories over his casket. Again, there was no official farewell.

That avoidance of death continued well into my marriage. I politely declined to accompany my husband to funerals, even those of family or close friends. *Not once* did I attend a funeral until I was in my late twenties, and it wasn't because there was a moratorium on deaths from those two decades either. Let's just go ahead and put my relationship with funerals and dying into the "unhealthy" category, shall we?

No song, no consolation, and no words really expressed my profound fear.

Three weeks after I gave birth to our third child, the call came in about Scott's dad. As a lifelong smoker, Bryant had been sick for years with heart and respiratory issues, and he had been hospitalized a number of times. The one time I visited him there, the antiseptic smell of the hospital soap and the sight of IVs was overwhelming. I had to excuse myself to the hallway to take a deep breath. As we made plans to visit him one last time, I cradled my newborn knowing I was going to have to dig deep. Looking back, I can see the beauty of him living long enough to meet his first granddaughter. But in that moment, I was just so fearful of seeing death up close and personal. To be honest, I was grateful that nursing and tending to a new baby gave me an excuse to gracefully exit some of the hardest milestones prior to, and following, his death.

A few years later, my husband's administrative assistant died unexpectedly, and Scott was asked to take part in the visitation and funeral. He eagerly agreed. When your mom and dad are the babies of twelve and thirteen children, respectively, death is a natural part of your childhood. Scott and I arrived at the funeral home, and he motioned for me to come kneel and pray before the casket. *Hell no*, I thought. Everyone kept saying things like, "Doesn't she look great?" or "That's just how I remember her." And all I could think is, *You're standing next to a dead body. Who does that and thinks it's normal?*

But in the fall of 2015, the rubber finally met the hot, Texas road.

It was a crisp, fall-like September day. I had recently broken my kneecap and was hopped up on pain meds, with my knee in a brace, hanging out on the couch with my kids. My cell phone rang, and in an instant, my entire relationship with death shattered in a million pieces.

My dearest friend's sixteen-month-old son had suffered a tragic accident and was on life support. I hobbled to my closet, out of earshot of my children, slumped to the carpet, and began sobbing. At Mass that evening, I stood in the narthex with my own six-teen-month-old and begged God for a miracle. Our two babies, both the youngest of six, were born just three days apart at the same hospital and with the same nursing staff and obstetrician. The running joke between our two families was that these babies would eventually marry in Paris and we would pay for the wedding. When the news arrived the following day that he was gone, I felt completely hollowed out.

In the span of six weeks, our school community experienced a total of four tragic and painful deaths—my friend's toddler, a student, a young mother, and a beloved grandfather and school benefactor. We loaded up the kids and attended four visitations and funerals, and cooked dinners and consoled four families. I found myself at a loss for words. It was music and Jesus that gave words to my pain and rubbed a salve on my weary and heartbroken soul.

Before, I had always been able to make excuses, to worm my way out of dealing with death. But when one of your dearest friends is up against her biggest cross, you don't just send a card and some flowers.

Perhaps that was the part I had been missing all along. I had tried to avoid the pain because I believed there was no antidote. I had let my fear of the unknown blind me from seeing God's great merciful love, even in terrible loss.

Our school community gathered to pray the Rosary, and at the conclusion, one of the moms received a text message that the family needed lunch. I immediately volunteered. It wasn't until I rounded the corner to their house with bags of groceries that I realized how utterly unprepared I was to greet my friend, her husband, and their five beautiful children who were in the midst of their deepest sorrow.

As I slowly approached her house, I could feel the same fear that had encompassed me as I stood at Luke's NICU bedside, begging for him to live. I was also acutely aware of God's presence; his love was tangible, I could feel it. I whispered a simple *Come, Holy Spirit* as I put the van into park. And damn, if God didn't show up. As Marguerite and I stood in her front lawn, embracing for what seemed like an eternity, I felt God in a way I have only felt him one time before—at Luke's bedside, just after he stopped breathing. The days, weeks, and months that followed with Marguerite and her family opened up a new part of my heart, one I was unaware existed.

I knelt, with all six of my children and my husband, at the casket of that little boy. I kept questioning God. But I also kept showing up, agreeing to serve as a reader at that young mother's funeral. It was an opportunity for me to reshape my children's view of death and show them we can do hard things. I pray they will not run from death, as I did for so many years.

Death is a topic many of us skirt around, pretending that if we don't acknowledge it, suffering will never find us. Seeing the beautiful love outpoured on those four families made it possible for the thing I feared to turn into something that changed my perspective. Those four families allowed me to fully understand that when there is suffering, there is also grace. And the grace always outweighs it.

Always.

That grace wasn't just a fleeting emotion. It has remained and continued to transform me, particularly in my relationship with my last living grandparent.

I've always been close to my grandfather, perhaps because he lived near us growing up or maybe because he always had the best stories. Papa was a member of the Greatest Generation, surviving thirty-five missions as a tail gunner on a B-17 in World War II. The average B-17 crew flew between twelve and fourteen missions and had a 75 percent mortality rate. Tail gunners, however, had a life expectancy of two weeks, which equaled about four missions. My papa crash-landed twice and survived the war, miraculously, as a man filled with vivid stories and a refreshing perspective.

His first marriage ended in divorce. After thirty-one years, he could no longer endure the suffering of having a raging alcoholic as his wife. He and his second wife, Ollie, married about a decade later, and he was so very happy. She succumbed to cancer a few years later, but rather than becoming bitter, he started dancing and playing bridge. That's when he met Great Betty. She opened up a side of my grandfather that was filled with a zest for living.

They married in their late seventies, and at ninety, he buried Betty. A year later, just after making his meal plan for the week, prepping his four raised planting beds, and laying out his spring flowers, Papa died suddenly.

I was grossly unprepared for the enormity of that loss. We talked often, and every time someone celebrated a birthday in our household, we could count on a "Papa phone call." They would usually scream in the phone because his hearing went to pot after the war, but oh how they looked forward to his familiar "Is *this* the birthday kid?"

One afternoon I called him out of the blue. We chatted for ten minutes about nothing and everything. Just before we hung up, he observed, "Out of the one thousand, four hundred and forty minutes today, I sure am grateful you spent ten of them with me." I fought back the tears and told him how much I loved him. "I sure do love you more," he replied.

There are still two voicemails on my iPhone; I can't bring myself to delete them. The first is a quick "happy birthday" to one of the kids. In the other he shares how much he loves me and then spends the next minute and a half trying to figure out how to hang up the call. iPhones were never his forte.

Because my grandfather wasn't Catholic, there was no formal visitation the night before the funeral. Fortunately, the funeral home director and I were in high school youth group together, and the evening before the funeral, he invited me to come up and spend a few final minutes before they closed the casket. Scott accompanied me, and as I gazed at Papa's strong frame, admired his weathered face, and thanked God for the gift of his life, I was struck at just how far my relationship with death had come. Years earlier, I wouldn't have gone near a casket. But now I stood before him with confidence and love, fully appreciating the journey instead of shying away from the reality of loss.

We knelt beside his casket, and Scott prayed a decade of the Rosary. In that moment I finally felt the peace come flooding in. At the funeral and burial the following morning, there was great sorrow—of course—but it was joined with sweeping gratitude.

It's a poignant reminder that all points of our life intersect. Luke's brush with death opened my eyes to the preciousness of life. The death of our friend's young son showed me how to embrace another's suffering. The passing of my grandfather allowed me to be fully present and willingly walk into the pain as we witnessed the close of his earthly chapter.

How, though? How do we embrace the suffering, the death, and the pain so willingly? Gratefully even?

"You have to learn to love the bomb," says funnyman and late-night host Stephen Colbert. He's witty and astute, and what Catholic doesn't chuckle while watching his liturgical dance rendition of "King of Glory"? (Google it and thank me later.) Before his late-night show launched in 2015, *GQ* magazine did an interview with him. What struck me about it most was how the tragedy of his background—his father and two brothers closest to him in age were killed in a plane crash when he was ten—actually helped him to fully embrace the joy of living. Over time and through the example of his mother, he became grateful for the thing he feared the most.

The Letters of J.R.R. Tolkien expresses a similar sentiment, that divine "punishments" are also divine "gifts." It's when we dive into the depths of pain and suffering that we develop an intimacy with God that is learned in no other way. We see how "the bomb" of great and unimaginable suffering changes us. We are permanently altered but, if we choose, also grateful. Perhaps I need to affix the same note on my computer that Colbert has taped to his: "Joy is the most infallible sign of the existence of God."

When I worked for the National FFA Organization, I had the privilege of searching for and booking our national convention speakers. One in particular, Gerda Klein, was a Holocaust survivor. Her book *All But My Life* tells her harrowing story of loss, desperation, hope, joy, and finally, love. When I met her, I was struck by how filled she was with absolute and total joy. It was undeniable. Her catastrophic loss hadn't taken away her soul because she didn't allow it. In her book, she shares, "My experience has taught me that all of us have a reservoir of untapped strength that comes to the fore at moments of crisis."

Our son, funerals, and really being present to those enduring excruciating pain? Those are the bombs I've learned to love. I'm not interested in being bitter: a party of one. Instead, I prefer to be grateful for it all—the pain and suffering as well as the joy and redemption. I don't wish for death and suffering, but I am unashamedly, fully, and joyfully grateful for all of it. In the end, it's because we are *this* because of *that*.

My epiphany of "this because of that" came, providentially, through music. Not long after the tragedies in our school community and the passing of my grandfather, a familiar song came on the radio, Brandon Heath's "Love Never Fails." I was sitting behind an ambulance, emergency transporting a newborn to the children's hospital, and Brandon's lyrics were a balm to my broken and healing heart.

> Love is not proud
> Love does not boast
> Love after all
> Matters the most

Love will protect
Love always hopes
Love still believes
When you don't

Love is the arms that are holding you
Love never fails you

Music put to words what my heart was unable to adequately express. As I sat behind that ambulance, blaring its lights and sounds, I felt a loving embrace from God. Brandon's words were a poignant reminder of how my love was revitalized and strengthened through all my encounters with death. God reminded me that while I couldn't take away the suffering, I couldn't mend the body, and I couldn't undo what was done, I could love.

The Kathryn who feared death finally matured and grew. That growth happened only when she allowed the fear and pain of yesterday to become her strength for today and her hope for tomorrow.

All along, the answer to my fear of death had been big love.

A **grateful heart** silences
a **complaining voice.**

★ *Bishop Eugene J. Gerber,*
Diocese of Wichita

Chapter 6

MAGIC
SOLUTION

Some might call me "structured."

It's the hazard of being the daughter of a school-teacher and a United States Army man. My closet is in rainbow color order, short sleeve to long. Each of my kids has a number and a designated color for things such as cups, bath towels, blankets, and toiletries. We have a magnetic meal calendar I update each month. My kids each have a storage box with folders labeled by grade; each contains all the memorable school projects and papers. It's accompanied by a baby book in their designated family color. I load the dishwasher the same way every night, and there is a right and a wrong way to fold towels. And I have labels—for everything. The freak flag of order flies high at our house.

In college, I was the same way. It just became more magnified with the entrance of six children. Chaos can reign, but order brings peace, right? With each child, I found myself obsessed with making the ship run smoothly.

A place for all the shoes so they were easy to store and find the following morning? Check. Bento boxes, in the designated color of course, lined up and ready for school lunches? Check. Colored toy bins with cute labels so both the younger kids and the older ones could put things back where they belong? Check. Pantry dry goods in clear containers, labeled for easy access? Check, check, check. At one point, every Monday, I dutifully posted a "how do you do it?" on my family blog, sharing tips on organization and order in our home. It was all good stuff, helpful even. Having order meant less stress, less stress meant more peace, and more peace meant more space for God.

But that order and illusion of peace came at a price.

I had always been organized, but Luke's arrival put it into hyperdrive. During his NICU stay when he stopped breathing, I did the only thing I knew how to do. I organized a notebook of medical files. It's what a type A mom who craves order does. It had pretty tabs for bills, insurance claims, and medical diagnosis summaries. It even had a cute cover, with "Luke's Medical Information" on paper framed in multicolored footprints. It gave me the illusion of control for about 0.05 seconds. As I sat in the corner of his nursery, I began to wonder what I else I could do or organize to make our life normal again.

I became fixated on ordering the things in our life that I could control because so much was spinning out of control with him. Each hospitalization would spur a new project once we returned home. We ripped out closets and repainted them, installing better storage solutions. I spent a crazy six hours sorting Legos by color and then putting them in the appropriate IKEA bin, with the instruction books all bound together so a set could be reassembled at a moment's notice (as if that ever happens!). I even went through old scrapbooks and culled bad photos to conserve space in the nursery closet. We won't even talk about how many hours that took. We re-sodded the yard, cleaned out the backyard shed, and decluttered the garage. Some of that was good and necessary. With a bustling house of six children, there must be time spent on order or you will literally lose your you-know-what. Ask me how I know.

It wasn't until years later, through prayer, time, and a crazy whole house purge that I finally recognized just how my fear of not being in control was manifesting itself in unhealthy ways. While some of the projects we took on brought greater peace to our home, some of them served as a mighty fine distraction to getting to the real heart of confronting my fear of not having it all together.

Scrolling through Instagram one January, I stumbled upon my friend Stephanie's post about embarking on a ten-day whole house purge and deep clean. I felt like a dog on a dove hunt. My ears perked up and I thought to myself, *I was born for this!* I assembled my boxes (donate, trash, recycle, and sell), gathered my cleaning supplies (even whipped up a batch of my own), and armed myself with paper towels and microfiber cloths. Seriously, y'all, this was right up my alley. We followed a plan outlined in a book by Tsh

Oxenreider, *Organized Simplicity*, which led us through decluttering and deep-cleaning various rooms in our house over the course of two weeks, taking the weekend off. Tsh's book encouraged readers to eliminate obvious visual clutter, empty the room, deep-clean it, and then load back in only what made sense.

I took no prisoners. Every two days, the minivan was filled with another collection of boxes of items we were selling, donating, or trashing. It was freeing. My ovens were the cleanest they had ever been, and the magic solution recipe to clean them naturally that I shared on social media became my most popular direct message. (It's 1 cup water, 1 tablespoon castile soap, and 10 drops lemon or orange essential oil, in case you're wondering.) On day five of the first week, a Friday night, Scott was standing atop a step stool polishing the kitchen cabinets, while I sorted through wedding gifts in our dining room hutch.

We were living our best life, and I'm positive Scott was thinking he had married up.

The first week I tackled the kitchen, dining room, playroom, laundry room, and living area. Week two was bathrooms, master bedroom, entryway, office, and the kids' rooms, including closets. I went in feeling tired but confident that I would finish strong. The kids told me I was nuts. They were on a mission to hunt down the mom that started this and give her a piece of their mind. Somehow we all rallied and I found myself in the nursery closet, near the end of the purge.

I had put it off long enough.

Luke's NICU boxes sat in the far corner of the closet. In it were all the itty-bitty clothes he wore in the early days, his discharge papers, admission bracelets, stacks and stacks of cards sent by friends and family, NICU paraphernalia, and even one of his tiny diapers. For a moment, I froze. The deep cleaning and the sorting had all seemed so freeing up to this point. It was fairly easy to disconnect myself from the "thing" while still holding on to the memory. But that box was different.

For nearly eight years, I had put off having to deal with the reality that lay in those boxes. It was time for the Kathryn who controlled every aspect of her life to submit herself to the unknown of what she may uncover—the feelings, the emotions, and the total loss of control.

I did what any rational human being would do. I sat in the middle of the floor, sobbed, and had a pity party.

Every hard day, every devastating diagnosis, every surgery, every excruciatingly long call to the insurance company, every setback, and every fear—it was all laid out in front of me in nice, color-coded, organized piles.

It was the first time that I allowed myself to fully mourn the loss of normal.

A good half hour and a box of Kleenex later, I dried my tears and began asking God just how I was going to move forward. One part of me wanted to put all those neat piles back in the boxes, seal them up, and put them right back on the shelf. But I had come too far. God had afforded me all those years of setting the fear aside because he knew I wasn't ready to face it head on. But staring at those boxes, I knew the day had come. It was time to confront my fears, lean into the pain and its many lessons, hold them tight one last time, and then let them go. I had to recognize the hardness of the past and send it packing so I could fully enjoy today.

I set aside my most favorite NICU outfit, recycled all the discharge papers, trashed the bills that had long been paid, kept a handful of cards, and lovingly wrapped up the remaining clothes. Somewhere in Austin, I knew there was a mother wondering what her preemie son's future looked like. Surely Luke's clothes could be put to good use instead of gathering dust. They were donated to our local children's hospital NICU. Giving them away was one of the hardest, most freeing things I've ever done.

That tiny pile of clothes felt like this monumental step forward. The next few days we finished the whole house purge (and then I drank two very cold Shiner Bock beers). Yes, the cobwebs were gone and my baseboards were sparkling, but it was my heart I set free. I had no idea that a challenge meant to free me of physical clutter would also clean out the boxes of guilt I stored deep within the recesses of my heart. The clothes were gone, but the treasured lessons remained, and I was affirmed in allowing God to transform me.

The more you purge, the less you have to take care of and the more time you have to spend doing things with people you love. The added bonus? Following the purge, we became more intentional about what we brought into our home. That led to greater financial freedom.

We live in an age where minimalism is celebrated. There are blogs and websites, ad campaigns, and HGTV programming dedicated to it. Celebrating the consumption of less has become a rallying cry for many. But had that minimalist attitude also pervaded my relationship with Christ? Had I sunk to doing the bare minimum in my desire to cultivate my faith? I finally asked myself some hard questions: *Am I minimalist Christian or an extravagant one? Have I minimized the material goods so that I can be abundant in giving and receiving Christ's love?*

During a Lenten parish mission, Fr. Emmerich Vogt, O.P., once relayed how all of his possessions were housed in a simple shoebox and how freeing it was. Confronting those NICU boxes in the closet opened my eyes to a greater purpose, as crazy as it may sound. By freeing myself of the physical clutter, I had made room for Jesus where it mattered—my soul. I finally had the space to see him at work in my life.

The Christmas season following the purge, we joined a dozen other families with trunks full of food, sacks of clothes (many from that purge), handfuls of gift cards, and hearts brimming with the joy of Christ's birth. My do-good attitude had the evening in downtown Austin all planned out in my mind. And then my daughter Anna-Laura spotted a familiar face among the homeless.

George was a homeless man we had the honor of working with at Community First! Village a few weeks prior. The village is the passionate apostolate of Alan Graham, founder of Mobile Loaves and Fishes and a revered champion of the dignity of the homeless. George had been one of the homeless on-site at the village, working alongside my children as they weeded and planted gardens. The residential program is unique in that the homeless in search of permanent residence are paired with volunteers to maintain the community. We offered a donation to Community First!, which in turn allows the residents to earn an income and pay rent for their housing at the village.

George's eyes brightened as he recognized the kids. And with a baby on my hip and no hesitation I asked him, "Do you mind if I give you a hug?" He nodded and tears filled his eyes. Encounters with Christ never cease to take my breath away.

The evening hadn't been about us or the homeless. It had been about God. When we detach ourselves from the physical clutter, releasing ourselves to be open to the will of God, we are given an opportunity. It's not enough to declutter and be good stewards of what you're given. Capsule wardrobes, organized Lego bins, and labeled pantry goods—they're all fine and dandy, but what are you sharing of yourself in the name of God? As Fr. Richard reminded us, it's time to get uncomfortable—like, hugging-a-homeless-man-in-a-parking-lot-in-downtown-Austin-with-a baby-on-your-hip uncomfortable.

In the US Bishops' Pastoral Letter on Stewardship, we are reminded that "*Jesus does not call us as nameless people in a faceless crowd*. He calls us *individually, by name*. . . . The challenge, then, is to understand our role—our vocation—and to respond generously to this call from God. Christian vocation entails the practice of stewardship" (emphasis mine).

The purge, the encounter, the contentment—it all sparked gratitude for every aspect of our life. Recently, we decided to get rid of our formal living room. We had multiple kids in school, and every night we found ourselves with homework overflowing on the kitchen table. The bedroom I had been using as an office became a bedroom once again, and that formal living space needed purpose other than looking pretty. The computers are all out in the open, and we decorated the space in white furniture, bright colors, beautiful fabric, and inspirational quotes.

Over the kids' computer area, I hand-painted one of our favorite quotes: *A grateful heart silences a complaining voice.* It was a gold nugget of a quote from an annual stewardship conference my husband attends.

Recognizing the goodness and generosity of people around us reemerged during our whole house purge. If comparison is the thief of joy, then gratitude and an awareness of just how rich in love we really are must be the cure.

I had allowed displaced order in my life to take the place of true and genuine joy—joy for the people in residence in my home, in what I owned, and in who God was creating me to be. Confronting the physical clutter forced me to choose joy and let order be the outgrowth of it, rather than the other way around.

I had to choose joy first, not order.

St. John Paul II reminds us, "To maintain a joyful family requires much from both the parents and the children. Each member of the family has to become, in a special way, the servant of the others."

My husband has been a fundraiser his entire professional career, raising money for universities, a youth organization, and two Catholic diocesan offices. He often tells me the number one reason people don't give is because they aren't asked. We make up their minds for them and decide if they can, or can't, give. Applying that mentality to my relationship with God, how many times have I refrained from asking God what he wants from me? My honest answer is almost every dang day. I decide, before ever asking him, what I am capable of giving and what I am capable of receiving.

It's a process of appreciating that stewardship and the giving of ourselves—time, talent, and treasure—isn't about how much we give but about how we joyfully give it.

In a society that lauds us for accumulating more, doing more, and being more, it's countercultural to hold up our hands in surrender and say, *no more*. Before the purge, I think I felt beholden—both consciously and subconsciously—to things.

Perhaps it's time for you to do a whole-soul purge. It really is possible to remove the barriers to a true and lasting relationship with God, to scrub clean our doubts, to feel worthy of love, and to seek joy. Maybe you'll deep-clean your oven and soak the grates in hot water and OxiClean, or maybe you'll find yourself in the confessional. Perhaps your closet will be organized in rainbow color order or you'll start to organize your day to leave room for God. You could take stock of your spice rack or take stock of your holy friendships. Or both.

A life of order is a good and holy endeavor. Just be careful about responding to a challenge on Instagram. You may come armed with trash bags, magic solution, and microfiber cloths, and walk away with a lighter heart, a happier home, and a joy-filled relationship with Christ.

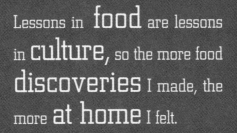

Lessons in food are lessons in culture, so the more food discoveries I made, the more at home I felt.

★ *Daniel Vaughn,*
TEXAS MONTHLY BBQ *editor*

Chapter 7

BBQ, SWEET TEA, AND A WHOLE LOTTA JESUS

When Scott and I married in 1996, we were living on a paltry $495 a month as graduate students at Iowa State. As in, the last week of every month meant eating peanut butter and jelly sandwiches. But we had a sense of adventure in us, and we often found ways to have fun for free, or pretty darn close to it.

As an intern for the Iowa State Foundation, one of Scott's perks was attending collegiate football games and eating for free in the fancy end-zone suite along with all of the donors. In the summers, we enjoyed fireworks near Reiman Gardens, sitting on the tailgate of Scott's pickup truck, and traveling around the state checking in with undergraduates doing their summer internships. Back then, it was always about the adventure.

To celebrate our first anniversary, we came up with enough money to drive to neighboring South Dakota. Our primary motivation for going was to see Mount Rushmore and the Badlands (incredibly impressive, by the way). It wasn't until late Saturday night that we remembered our Sunday Mass obligation. This was well before Google, but our trusty road map told us that Blessed Sacrament was the closest parish. It wasn't our intention to go to Mass on vacation since it was just a quick weekend jaunt. That commitment to seek out a church in Rapid City, South Dakota, though, began a tradition of us making it a point to attend Mass on vacation, no matter what.

On our first pilgrimage to Italy with the youth of our parish, we were really struggling with various Church teachings. A collision of vacation and faith began to take root in Italy. For the first time, we saw the intersection of them both, instigating a shift in how we practiced our faith once we returned home. Faith and life were no longer separate occurrences, where we paid polite homage to Jesus at Sunday Mass and then forgot to look for him the rest of the week. Rather, we started to see him all around us—in everything and in every place.

For years after that revelation in Rome, we felt as if attending Mass was all the Jesus we needed on vacation, but an unexpected trip to Europe began to shift our hearts, just before Luke was born. I left the other four children with family and met Scott at the end of his business trip, and we flew to France for the week. It was early in my pregnancy, still the first trimester, and while I was tired, I still felt adventurous. St. Thérèse was a new-to-me saint, and I was thrilled we would be driving right through her hometown of Lisieux on our way to the monastery at Mont-Saint-Michel in northern France.

Scott and I opened the door to the basilica in Lisieux just as the rector was walking out. "Bonjour!" he called out, smiling widely. Perhaps it was my Texan version of *bonjour* back to him, but he stuck out his hand and said, "Welcome to France, my American friends!" He invited us in and told us to enjoy the space. Scott and I, miraculously, were the only other people in this highly visited basilica. We lit our candles, and Scott knelt to pray. The jetlag was starting to catch up to me, so I simply sat on the pew, closed my eyes, and breathed in the cool air of the basilica's concrete walls.

It had been a hectic start to the trip. On top of the craziness in getting four kids back home situated for my absence, I was especially anxious about this pregnancy. Something seemed off, but I couldn't put my finger on it. The quiet church, the rhythm of my beating heart, and Scott's reassuring presence finally allowed the peace to creep in, slowly. What started all those years ago as a commitment to attend Sunday Mass on vacation was morphing into *this*—a full-fledged Scott-and-Kathryn pilgrimage to strengthen our faith.

God was preparing us for our biggest battle, and we didn't even know it.

We came home refreshed and renewed in our marriage—Sacré Cœur, La Tour Eiffel, filet de boeuf, the Louvre, PAUL croissants, and Avenue Montaigne will do that to you. However, six weeks later, at my twenty-week ultrasound, the boom lowered. And after Luke's birth we were squarely in the third circle of hell.

At ten months old, Luke was fresh off his fourth surgery (this time for his spine), and his sleeping was atrocious. He would spend hours screaming at night. With five kids ages eight and under, mounting medical bills, and the stress of Luke's therapy and specialist appointments, we were tapped out physically, emotionally, and financially. What a far cry from France, a mere year before.

After that hospital stay to correct Luke's spine, out of the blue a generous friend offered his house in Ruidoso, New Mexico, for the week, which meant that our only expenses would be food and the gas to get there and back. With a string of one-hundred-degree days on the horizon, a trip to enjoy New Mexico's cooler temperatures would be a figurative and literal escape from the pressure cooker of our current life. We said yes, while fully expecting the trip to be a massive fail.

As we pulled out of our driveway the next morning, kid number two started throwing up and registered a low-grade fever. We handed him a plastic bag, gave him some ibuprofen, and headed west. That tells you just how desperate we were to escape. I think I cried the first four hours of the drive, along with everyone else. To add a little extra icing on the cake, when we arrived at the house late that evening, the smoke detector was beeping (of course it was). God was not to be outdone in his mercy though. Two of my dad's high school classmates lived around the corner. Providentially, he texted just before we arrived and told me to reach out to them if we needed anything. Turns out, we needed an extension ladder and some batteries. After a frantic, late-night text to Young and Mike, they arrived moments later with an extension ladder, batteries, *and* beer. Fifteen minutes after they left, we had a working detector, cold beer, and four kids sound asleep. Yes, Luke was screaming his head off, but I counted surviving this ordeal as the first miracle of our trip.

Luke continued to wail throughout the night for the next five days, but something in our family shifted on that escape from the suffocating pressure of prematurity and life. We began to embrace the mess, taking to heart the lessons from our pilgrimages to Italy and France. Through the screaming, the high fever, and a blaring fire alarm, we started to discover our peace.

Deer fed in our front yard every morning while the kids ate their breakfast, listening to the self-playing piano in the entry. Yes, there was a grand piano that played classical music at the touch of a button. Nicely done, God. We went skidding down the piles of sand at White Sands National Park, learned about forest fires and Smokey the Bear, watched a horse race at Ruidoso Downs, and played a mean round of putt-putt. In the evenings, Scott prayed with the kids while I nursed Luke to sleep. We passed the long hours of screaming by reading Harry Potter and praying the Rosary. I knocked out the entire seven-book series in four days, a personal record.

We came back to Austin with renewed intention. Yes, we were still dog tired, but the respite we so desperately craved, God gave to us in spades. Vacations went from being an escape from real life to an opportunity to *really live life* with Jesus.

Luke was sleeping mildly better the following summer, so we decided to take another leap and drive from

Texas to the Florida Panhandle to spend time with my brother, his wife, and their daughter in Destin. Along the way, we celebrated Mass with our dear friend Archbishop Aymond in New Orleans and then stopped to reconnect with college friends in Gulfport, Mississippi. We even ran into my college roommate just outside of Destin, on the beach. Yes, we had encountered God at churches and pilgrimage sites, but we now started looking for him in the smallest of places.

We doused the kids with Holy Water as we began our drive each morning (they complain about getting soaked, but we do it anyway) and offered prayers at rest stops for our meals. And on particularly difficult stretches—in an effort not to disown all our offspring—we asked for intentions from friends to focus our prayers.

The hours in the van are not always idyllic. There are still sibling fights—save me, Jesus, from the bickering—and usually at least one "Don't make me pull this van over" (and we typically do). But there is purpose. There is intentionality in the journey and a whole lot of living in between.

During our 'Merica tour (also known as the *certifiably bananas excursion*), we hit nine states in eight days. We began with my niece's Baptism in Dallas and then hit Kansas, Missouri, Illinois, Indiana, Kentucky, Tennessee, Mississippi, and Louisiana. The boys donned albs to be altar servers at a beautiful church in Westfield, Indiana. Our decision to try daily Mass, however, was a massive fail. One would think attending anything for twenty minutes is possible, but not if you're a kid whose last name is Whitaker.

Even amid the apparent fails, however, we sought out the joy. There was picnicking on the grounds of our Indiana parish with our middle child Clare's godfather, our former parish priest, and a godmother; taste-testing bourbon in Kentucky (that counts as spiritual, right?); swinging real Louisville Slugger bats (where no one was injured—a miracle!); visiting the Grand Ole Opry in Nashville; and touring the site of the Battle of Vicksburg in Mississippi. But it was in Louisiana that Clare stole the show. When we rolled up to Popeye's for a quick lunch, she yelled out, "Oh! It's Pope Yes!" Jesus on vacation? Nailed it.

Our West Coast trek during the Year of Mercy was sanctifying. A good thirty-seven hours in the van and a small scare with the radiator overheating in Devil's Canyon (I swear, I can't make this stuff up) meant occasional sibling fights, but it also meant spending real quality time with people we adored—a college friend, family, and internet friends turned real-life ones. We said simple prayers of thanksgiving in a rural Texas church. We survived Mass with a fussy toddler and received a blessing at San Juan Capistrano in California. And we witnessed the tangible wonder of the Grand Canyon and the Lower Antelope slot canyons on our twentieth wedding anniversary. Scott and I were thrilled to stand on the corner in Winslow, Arizona, (the Eagles would be proud) and share a kiss. Surprisingly, the kids did not share our joy.

I think it's the five thousand miles we've clocked in Texas alone, though, that have been my favorite. It's amazing what a mom will do for a cold beer. Or in my case, a cooler to ensure that the beer is extra cold.

It all started thanks to our love of barbecue and a YETI cooler. Every four years, the state magazine *Texas Monthly* publishes its Top 50 BBQ list. The barbecue editor—yes, that's a real thing—Daniel Vaughn, and his team scour the state looking for the best 'cue. They endure months of taste-testing tender ribs, savory beans, and mouth-watering brisket meals all in the name of "the best Texas barbecue." For those who took the challenge of visiting all fifty stops on the list, YETI (the Mercedes-Benz of coolers) rewarded barbecue aficionados with a slew of coolers, drinkware, buckets, and accessories worth about $1,500.

After reading the barbecue issue and perusing our vacation route around the Lone Star state, Scott and our boys Will and John Paul had mapped out—unbeknownst to me—all the joints along our driving route. I figured one place would be fine, but there was no need to go overboard—that is, until I took a bite of some south Texas chicken tortilla soup (made with smoked chicken) and dove into Tex-Mex-inspired chicken enchiladas. Then and there, I decided this barbecue pilgrimage was happening.

As much as I love me some good barbecue, hauling all six kids around the state to sample the top fifty joints in Texas seemed insane. But the call of brisket and sweet tea was strong, y'all. Following that week-long vacation where we got a taste of some great joints, we spent the next nine months in search of the very best. Lucky for us, nearly a dozen are within an hour of Austin (Valentina's, Franklin's, La Barbecue, and Stiles Switch are some of our local favorites).

In our quest to eat really exceptional barbecue, we also found a whole lotta Jesus. I suppose it started as a food challenge before it barreled through crazy and ended up as a true pilgrimage, both gastronomically and spiritually speaking. Our ten-month Texas barbecue tour fed not only our bellies but also our souls. Daniel Vaughn was right. The food gave us a lesson in culture and led us to experience some amazing spiritual moments. We began to feel even more at home in our state, in our family, and in our faith. Barbecue encouraged us to hit the road, while Jesus met us at every single stop—proof that he loves brisket and ribs as much as we do, right?

We enjoyed lighting candles, praying for others, going to confession, and listening to the mariachi band at a Lenten Mass at the Basilica of Our Lady of San Juan del Valle. We received a wedding blessing at a Sunday Mass in the tiniest church in Marfa, population 1,724. Knowing we were visitors, the priest hauled us up to the front while the entire congregation witnessed his blessing on us for more than two decades of marriage. We made a pit stop in Shiner (home of Shiner Bock beer), but not before making time to visit the local church and pray before the Tabernacle. I'm also certain our future cause for canonization was furthered when we visited three barbecue joints in Houston on a Friday during Lent and didn't eat a single bite of meat. We just packed it all in our YETI coolers and ate it on Saturday morning for breakfast!

The destination is always important, but it's relationships along the way that change us. The people we meet on the journey are always the very best part. The road there changes and challenges us to step outside of our preconceived ideas of how great God is and to really experience his big, bountiful love. The final destination is just barbecue sauce on the brisket.

Hawaii is on our bucket list, and it appears that's where it will stay for a while. With six kids and no money tree in the backyard, how do we provide our kids with the storybook childhood of vacations and "life experiences"? Answer: We stopped overdoing it. We quit trying to make family memories extra fabulous and instead made them extra genuine.

There have been multiple trips around Texas that didn't include barbecue, but they did involve Buc-ee's (the Disneyland of gas stations), visits to Central Texas's painted churches, South Texas basilicas, San Antonio missions, Houston cathedrals, Panhandle cemeteries, and various pilgrimage sites. During confession at one of those churches, I was lamenting to the priest how I was starting to lose my virtue-that-shall-not-be-named with the kids. We'd spent one too many hours in the minivan. I could hear him laughing on the other side of the screen. He asked if I prayed the Rosary and then encouraged me to do one simple thing the next time I prayed. "When you pray the Hail Mary, pause five to ten seconds just before you say 'Jesus.' Give that name pause, and ask for him to grant you the patience when you need it, especially in our fast-paced, distracted world." That was his advice.

> Hail Mary, full of grace, the Lord is with thee. Blessed art thou among women and blessed is the fruit of thy womb . . . [pause] Jesus.
>
> Holy Mary, mother of God, pray for us sinners, now and at the hour of our death.

You exhaled, didn't you? Every time I feel rushed, those wise words echo in my mind and I pause. And y'all, that advice didn't even cost me a plane ticket to Hawaii!

Part of finding your peace in life is being intentional. Individual time with our children isn't an afterthought for us; it's a central theme. Our family celebrates each kid's tenth birthday with great fanfare because of two other families who inspired us. The child gets to choose the parent and the destination, which must include a plane trip to one of the forty-eight contiguous states.

My eldest daughter, Anna-Laura, chose me and Chicago, Illinois. Our agenda included the big staples—Willis Tower, high afternoon tea at the Peninsula Hotel, deep-dish pizza at Gino's East, the Chicago Art Institute, Mass at Holy Name Cathedral, American Girl, the infamous Portillo's Hot Dogs, the Chicago Architectural Foundation boat tour, and of course the Science and Industry Museum. The big and grand moments were many, but it was after dinner one night, walking past a half dozen homeless men and women, that Anna-Laura's kind eyes implored mine.

"Mom, they look cold. Do you think we can buy them some socks?"

We found a CVS pharmacy a half block away, and armed with a dozen pair of socks, and hearts warm with love, I watched Anna-Laura pass out a pair to every homeless person we met. Amazingly, we bought exactly enough socks to give to every person we saw who needed them. If only you could've seen those weathered and hardened faces soften as she leaned down to each person, smiled, and said, "Would you like a pair of warm socks?"

Anna-Laura respected their dignity when she looked past their homelessness and saw them for who they were. Here I was planning a fancy tea at the nicest hotel and worrying about how we were going to make it from the American Girl doll store to Ghirardelli's before Mass, but she saw something different. While I'd like to think it's because of superior parenting, the credit is all God's. Kids haven't put up walls and they haven't crafted distractions to the beauty—or the need—right in front of them. Anna-Laura's kind heart reminded me to continue to look for Jesus all around me. As it turns out, on that trip to Chicago, he needed warm socks.

That wasn't the first time one of my own children ministered to me on vacation. On our East Coast trek to Washington, DC, we were in heavy traffic. After a jam-packed morning of touring, we ate lunch on the go to get to our next destination in time. A red light caused us all to take a much-needed deep breath when from the back of the van came the sweetest voice.

"Hey Dad, don't we have some extra sandwiches? We should give that guy something to eat."

As residents of a big city, panhandlers and home-lessness are part of our daily lives. But on vacation, I think it slipped my mind to be aware of those same trials in new and unfamiliar surroundings. The kids were quick to gather food from the back of the van to pass it forward for Scott to hand out. "God bless you, brother," I heard him say.

The photos we have of us visiting all the amaz-ing monuments and museums in DC are grand and they bring back fabulous memories, but there is one photo from the trip that put our "East Coast pilgrim-age" into perspective. We stayed with our friends, Mary and Jerry, in Fairfax, Virginia. When we arrived, they asked if we wanted to join them at their daughter's gravesite to plant flowers. Courtney suffered from an unknown seizure disorder that eventually took her life at twenty-two years old. On a warm evening in July, "bury the dead," a corporal work of mercy, took on a very personal and deeply sacred meaning. I had one kid screaming about the mosquitos, another petrified of getting dirty, and four working diligently to plant the flowers "just so." It was a unique honor to be trusted to beautify the graveside of someone's beloved. The experience changed our tone on that trip from exhaustion to gratitude.

Social media likes to feed us the lie that truly fabulous family vacations take us to exotic and frame-worthy places such as Bali and the Orient or romantic destinations such as Santorini or Venice. It's not really possible to find such beauty and meaning on the streets of Chicago; at the Maker's Mark distillery; on the side of the road in Marfa, Texas; or at a graveyard next to a tiny church in Fairfax.

Or is it? Don't sell God short. He has a unique way of finding us at every single mile marker along the way.

I'm quite positive that thousands of miles and countless hours in the van have been not only opportunities for sanctification (we won't get into pulling the van over somewhere near Atlanta, Georgia, and screaming at one another) but they have also been a gift to grow in faith and in relationship. I'm not referring to the self-serving martyrdom of road trips here. I'm talking about seeing the gift it is to spend that kind of time with the people in your life you deeply love.

About one day into every road trip, I always wonder if it was the worst idea ever dreamed by man. But the imperfect time away has the ability to show us, in a real and tangible way, that life is chaotic and unpredictable and God is right there in the middle of it.

In Pope Francis's apostolic exhortation *Evangelii Gaudium*, he speaks about "the art of accompaniment." In other words, it's not just about going somewhere with someone but rather about how present you are to one another along the journey. The destination is of no real measure or consequence if you haven't set your heart on Christ.

When I was a little girl, my grandfather, Papa, would take me on long drives from city to city in the Texas Panhandle. His pipe was perched on the dashboard, and he smelled like pressed tobacco, a deeply rich and inviting smell, unlike the bitterness of a cigarette. I remember the familiar smack as he would puff on his pipe. Before he set it in the dashboard holder, he would use it to point at something along our drive. Sometimes it was the discreet marker along Highway 287, affixed to an old barbed-wire fence, that marked the designation between Moore and Potter County (as an adult, I still look for those along every country road). Other times it was the cotton, just starting to mature, or a line of tumbleweeds threatening to roll across the road. He was full of stories, and he knew a little bit about almost everything.

The last time we took a drive together, Papa had recently celebrated his ninetieth birthday, and we were on our way to the cemetery to bury his third wife. He had already outlived the other two. He asked that I drive him and no one else accompany us. He wanted some "Kathryn time," as he called it. When you're ninety, you get to call the shots. We talked about my kids, my writing, struggling family members, and how he was doing. As we pulled into the deserted cemetery to bid our final good-byes to his beloved Betty, he squeezed my hand and winked. We hadn't driven down a particularly scenic highway, nor were we going anywhere exotic or magazine-worthy. Yet that drive was one filled with holy purpose. We accompanied one another that day; he was near the end of the road, and I was somewhere in the middle.

A year later, I found myself on that same road, accompanying my mom as we buried Papa in the family plot in the tiny Panhandle town of Perryton. There's a lot of highway up there, with nothing but the horizon in front of you, speckled with herds of cattle, farmland, irrigation units, and the occasional batch of tumbleweeds. The drive gave me time to reflect on the greatness of my grandfather's life. There, in the bright Texas sun, I stood over people who shaped Papa, who in turn shaped me. The expanse of that Panhandle horizon was no match for my grateful heart and the joy of the journey.

Sometimes our travel takes us to the places of our dreams, and sometimes it serves to remind us of who we are and where we came from. Our family excursions have rarely taken us to exotic places, but they have reconnected us with people we adore and given us new relationships to cherish. The everyday holy is real, we just have to open our eyes to appreciate it.

Whatever road life has paved for you, consider this: Forget about the destination and focus on the journey. Wherever you go, do it with intention and purpose. Travel with a heart anxious for accompaniment. And remember that the drive is always sweeter when Jesus is riding shotgun with you.

A girl should be two things:
classy and fabulous.

★ Coco Chanel

Chapter 8

THE HUSTLE IS
SOLD SEPARATELY

✦ ✦ ✦

Classy and *fabulous*. Two words I would not have said about my body back in 2009. To be completely transparent, I am still working on believing them wholeheartedly today. Learning to love yourself is a slow process of letting go of unrealistic expectations and who others think you should be—skinny, fit, organized, and patient all the time.

Women around the world are bombarded with the "perfect body image" on a daily basis through social media, billboards, and print and television ads, and I am no exception. My own negative body image began in fourth grade, at the young age of nine, with scoliosis, the lateral curve of the spine. For five and a half years—seventh grade to junior year—I wore a Boston

back brace for twenty-three hours a day, only removing
it to shower. The silver lining is that this was the 1980s
where oversized shirts were the fashion inspiration, so
I got really good at hiding it. As a coping mechanism, I
developed a wicked sense of humor. No one can make
fun of the kid cracking jokes if she always beats you
to the punch line (Class of 1992's "Most Witty," right
here, y'all).

Living with scoliosis and wearing that back brace
was a daily reminder that I was different, malformed
in some way, and not quite perfect. In middle school,
when girls began to size each other up and boys started
to take notice, I was sporting hard plastic, a baggy shirt,
and a permed bob. While that awkward stage kept me
out of most of the tween drama, it also cemented the
notion that I would never be good enough.

That negative self-image affected my dating, my
confidence, and my relationships with others. To make
matters worse, during my sophomore year in high
school we moved from the tiny Texas Panhandle town
I grew up in surrounded by understanding friends to
a bigger city where I knew no one.

In high school, the boys always saw me as their
bestie but never their girlfriend. Well, there was that one
guy who asked me to prom who ended up dealing mar-
ijuana—thankfully, that relationship was short-lived. I
was the resident relationship advice giver. Who really
wants to date the band nerd who wears a back brace?
My junior year, I was discharged from wearing that con-
strictive back brace for good. The "celebration outfit" I
wore is still crystal clear in my memory—a white shirt,
tucked in to my acid-washed jeans, finished off with
a hot pink satin ribbon belt. Be jealous, because I was

quite the fashionista. For one day I caught a glimpse of what it felt like to be self-assured, 1990 permed bob and all. It would be years before I felt that way again. If only I could tell high school Kathryn how wearing that brace would eventually reshape not only her spine but also her attitude, her soul, and her outlook on internal and external beauty.

For almost twenty years, the effects of the brace were largely successful. Shortly after the birth of my third baby, however, I was experiencing severe back pain and shortness of breath. At age thirty-four, an appointment with a spine surgeon revealed the severity of my curve; it was an astounding sixty-five degrees where it should have been zero. The curve would only worsen with time, and my spinal twist was already beginning to compress my internal organs. I elected to undergo major spinal surgery (my doctor called it open heart surgery for the back), just a day after I weaned my third baby. Nine hours in the operating room later, I was the proud owner of two titanium rods and twenty-four screws, with a fused spine from T-2 to L-1. Before operating, my surgeon asked if I had good walking shoes. "Movement is what will heal you," he reminded me. "The sooner you move, the quicker you'll be back to normal."

I was in the ICU for two days and have two painful, vivid memories. Being rolled on my side for x-rays just hours post-op, and then being asked to sit in a chair a few days later. Both had me screaming for Dilaudid, the strongest painkiller in the ICU. Once I was transferred from the ICU to the general floor, Scott gave me my first hospital shower as I sat on the shower stool, shivering and sobbing. I was broken, and this sure felt like hell's biggest pity party.

After surgery I thought, for sure, I would love my body now that I had a (mostly) straight spine. Instead, I was bitter that this was my life. The first week home plunged me back into life as a mom. The kids still needed to eat, take baths, and be loved. My limited physical mobility and excruciating pain meant I could only do the latter. After a horrifying first few days of sleep, Scott held my face in his hands and lovingly said, "Quit being a baby. You're the strongest person I know." Then he laced my tennis shoes and helped me make my first painful walk around the block. It took a half hour, and I came home sweaty, exhausted, and in horrible pain. Scott smiled triumphantly as we walked in the door, so much so that I almost punched him (except, excruciating pain). "That's the worst it will ever be," he said, and then squeezed my hand.

He was right.

And so began my daily routine for the next several months. I put on my shoes, charged my iPod, and walked. Brandon Heath, George Strait, Rascal Flatts, TobyMac, Neil Diamond, Justin Timberlake, the Spice Girls, and Jesus—they walked miles and miles with me, giving me time to think, to pray, and to heal. In the middle of the night, when the pain would wake me, music and prayer closed the gap until I could take another pain pill. Eventually, it was just the music and God, without the hydrocodone. My full physical recovery took a year.

Two years and two months post spinal surgery, I gave birth to our fourth child. My pregnancy was so very different with her. My straighter spine gave me an additional two inches in height, and I could finally breathe with a baby in there! Clare was a dream baby—eating and sleeping just like the books said she would. And I was feeling so very good about my physical self. Aside from my fourteen-inch scar and some permanent nerve loss in my back, I could finally stand up tall.

Stella had finally found her groove.

In my extreme arrogance, I could almost hear the words in my head being spoken out loud: *Clearly, I am doing motherhood right.*

Luke's premature birth tipped all that on its head.

His emergency C-section delivery left me with an unwanted scar, a flabby midsection, and a U-Haul's worth of guilt, shame, and disgust over my new body. It was hard to shake the lie, believing that my body had failed, even though I knew it was irrational. My C-section scar was a physical reminder of the heaviness and the weight of life since his birth. Most days, I was climbing out of the black cloud of all that felt impossible, but I got so very good at faking it to friends and family. Luke spent his first year undergoing surgeries and then years enrolled in intense physical, speech, and feeding therapy while I continued to struggle with how I felt and looked.

Four years after his birth, we welcomed our sixth baby. In the two years following that last pregnancy, I was slammed with health-related issues—a broken kneecap and the removal of several benign tumors. *Sheez, Jesus, give me a break here.* My self-confidence about my body and just how "beautiful" it was officially tanked. During months and months of physical therapy for my broken kneecap, working to regain flexibility and rebuild my quad muscle, I began to rethink just how much I was taking care of my physical self.

Enough was enough.

I could either hop on the pity bus or the hustle bus. I chose hustle and enrolled myself in a group fitness class, Pure Barre. For the record, I hated the thought of group fitness and being judged by women who I believed were succeeding at taking care of themselves much better than I was. Desperation spurs change, though, so I did it anyway.

My first class, one of the women beamed after a workout and said, "I'm so addicted to this workout. It's awesome!" I thought she might be on some illegal substance. I hated the class, primarily because it exposed just how weak I was in so many areas—back, core, quads, and upper body. Her comment made me feel that much more defeated. But because I am stubborn as hell and had paid for a month, I was determined to get my money's worth. Class by class, week by week, I began to notice a change. I stopped looking in the mirror at everyone else and instead saw my own reflection—a stronger, more confident version of myself. What began as an effort to rebuild a knee and lose some inches became more about my personal strength, my clear mind, and genuine friendships with other women in that room. The struggle bus became the victory bus—yes!

Our kids even noticed my commitment to regular exercise, and Scott was my biggest cheerleader. More important than his compliments was his desire to make sure we both had time to dedicate to our physical selves. When my alarm blared at 5:25 a.m., he was kind enough to shove me out of bed. The mindset was shifting in our home, and it surprised even me, the biggest skeptic of them all.

In high school I was the uncoordinated geeky band nerd who cracked jokes and was totally nonathletic. I thought a physically active lifestyle was something meant for other people, certainly not me. I wrongly assumed you had to be a seasoned athlete, an accomplished dancer, or a dedicated marathoner to be worthy of exercising. This and other lies we tell ourselves, right?

Scott's encouragement came fresh off the heels of Exodus 90—an intense ninety-day period of prayer, fasting, and asceticism supported by a small group of like-minded men. When I say intense, I mean it. For ninety days he took cold showers; cut out alcohol, dessert, Coke, television, movies, and material purchases; only listened to Christ-centered music; spent time on his computer for work only; engaged in regular exercise; and got at least seven hours of sleep a night. He also met weekly with his small group. He jokingly tells me it was one really long Lent! At first I was supportive, and by "supportive" I mean that I popped the top of my Dr Pepper can in front of him and told him how proud I was of his effort. I'm sure he appreciated my empathy. But Scott's dedication to a changed lifestyle meant a new style of leadership in our home, and it greatly affected me. *I* started to get serious too, which meant with two parents committed to a healthy lifestyle, the kids really jumped aboard the bandwagon.

Our older four children were already running cross-country, and to show them that mom was "really serious" about fitness, I signed up for a 5K with the neighborhood gals. Even though my time was a

ridiculously long forty-four minutes, when I crossed
the finish line, our kids cheered me on as if I had won.
John Paul, our born athlete who runs a 6:15 mile, con-
gratulated me with a "Good job, Mom. At least you've
got nowhere to go but up!"

God doesn't ask us to be perfect; he asks us to try.
Prior to Luke's birth, I wasn't trying. Shoot, prior to
any of the births of our six kids I wasn't trying. I wasn't
even treading water; I was just sitting on the side of the
pool complaining that I didn't know how to swim. We
don't have to be Olympians, just mindful of these wise
words from 1 Corinthians 6:19–20: "Do you not know
that your body is a temple of the holy Spirit within you,
whom you have from God, and that you are not your
own? For you have been purchased at a price. Therefore
glorify God in your body."

For you have been purchased at a price.

Women spend a lot of time worrying about what
other women think of them. What does God think? He
loves us, just as we are—absolutely. He also asks that
we become active participants in our own lives. Scripture tells us to glorify God in our bodies; it doesn't say
that he is only glorified if we wear size six or are an
ultra-marathoner. He asks us to wake up each morning
and begin again. There are days when I will eat chocolate for breakfast and drink beer for dinner (raise your
hand if you've done it). But there are many more days
when I strive to glorify God with how I treat this temple
I've been given. There's no Target ninety-day refund
here, y'all. This is all you get. It's a final sale.

Some of us are slow learners. God got my attention
with a bad back, a premature infant, and a broken kneecap. How is he trying to get yours? About a year after

I began working out regularly, I stood in the dressing room of my favorite store. Both my tween girls, Anna-Laura and Clare, accompanied me on the shopping trip and were excited to help me find "the one." Shopping for new clothes isn't something we do too terribly often, so this was definitely a treat. I was mulling over my four choices for a fancy dress that needed to double as both an Easter dress and as a first Communion dress for our youngest son's big day. One was black in all the right places, punctuated with big, beautiful flowers. Another was a little out of my comfort zone, but the mannequin in the window wore it so well, so maybe I could too. The third was a last-minute grab because it was on sale. The fourth was a lacy, white dress that was gorgeous, which meant it probably wouldn't fit.

As I slipped on the black dress, my oldest daughter, Anna-Laura, blurted out, "Mom, why are your hips so big?" Emphasis on the *so*. God love tweens and their astute observations. "Mom?" Anna-Laura said again, with a raised eyebrow. Her comment jolted me back to reality. In the early days of motherhood, I'm positive that statement would've sent me home in tears. Or at the very least, I would have scolded my daughter for voicing such an insensitive comment.

It's a gift to grow in maturity—usually—but it's almost always freeing. I smiled, hugged her, and said, "Babe, I earned these hips birthing you and your five siblings! Someday, I hope you can see their beauty too." What I really wanted to say is, "Hey, your dad likes them, and that's enough for me." But I chose the former.

She half smiled and said matter-of-factly, "Well, your hips don't look good in that one." She was right.

In fact, all the dresses made me a little hippy, except that white one. Turns out it did fit.

Women around the world—in every country, in every neighborhood, and of every race—struggle with body image. I am 100 percent convinced of it. It's not just the plunging necklines or the barely there hemlines that are vying for our fashion attention either. I'm sure Brené Brown, author and research professor studying courage, vulnerability, shame, and empathy, would agree that #fitspo shames in a whole new way, doesn't it?

"Fitsporation" has women posing on sites such as Instagram dressed in workout gear, smiling confidently so we can admire their toned abs, glutes, and biceps. The message of "suck it up now, so you don't have to suck it in later" is palpable. Who else has glanced down at her soft midsection or cellulite-ridden thighs and shaken her head in shame and defeat? Wait, don't answer that.

Instead of believing we were made in the "image and likeness of God," a lot of us think that God somehow gave us a lemon of a body. We clearly aren't working hard enough (or we are, and nothing is happening). He couldn't *really* love us unless we have the perfect body mass index and look great in all our clothes. Maybe he loves our brains and our hearts, but he definitely does not love our muffin top, right? We forget that love was already given, on the Cross, on the side of the hill, among a crowd filled with sinners.

In Romans 8:38, St. Paul reminds us, "For I am convinced that neither death, nor life, nor angels, nor principalities, nor present things, nor future things, nor powers, nor height, nor depth, nor any other creature will be able to separate us from the love of God in Christ Jesus our Lord."

Could we also add, "nor scales, nor tight jeans, nor warped full-length mirrors, nor carbs can separate us from God's love"?

It's a lesson I'm working on instilling in our girls, especially my daughter Clare. She was recently diagnosed with scoliosis. I noticed the familiar curve and promptly took her to my spine surgeon. Clare is currently sporting her own back brace to correct the curvature. After crying in my closet for a good half hour when the official diagnosis came in, I dug out my big-girl panties, hugged Clare tight, and thanked God for all those long and extraordinarily difficult years I spent in a brace.

As much as I want to take it from her, God is giving me another opportunity to walk the path of suffering with Clare and help her find redemption and peace with the body God has gifted her. All those years I doubted what the pain, discomfort, and teasing was for, I now see clearly. It was to show my daughter what real beauty looks like, and it isn't on the cover of *Shape* magazine. British princess Eugenie reminded us of this on her wedding day when she chose to wear a gown that revealed her own scoliosis surgery scar.

Austin has a plethora of specialists who are fellowship trained in pediatric scoliosis. Fortunately, my spine surgeon is also Clare's doctor, and he is an absolute rock star. He has made her experience positive, and her teachers have lifted her spirits, while her friends have rallied around her. I hope Amazon Prime still sells acid-washed jeans because we will have some celebrating to do in a few years. This time, though, I think we'll skip the perm.

Body image, and my love-hate relationship with my body, really came down to one thing: Do I believe I am worthy of being loved? Because if I believe that, then I have the strength and the fortitude to love myself and the people in my life. I have the power to become stronger—physically, emotionally, and spiritually. And I have the power to never wear high-waisted acid-washed jeans again. Perhaps I need to say it with a little more gusto—*you are enough, sister*. You are loved and seen by a God who desires only good for you.

Stop sitting on the sidelines and wishing for a new life. Wake up tomorrow, feeling classy and fabulous, and get busy glorifying God with your body. Just be sure to cancel your perm appointment. You'll thank me later.

Don't try to win over
the haters, you're not the
jackass whisperer.

★ *Scott Stratten,*
UNMARKETING

Chapter 9

AND OTHER LIES
WE TELL OURSELVES

✦ ✦ ✦

"Oh, you must be the *old* kindergarten mom," the perky twenty-six-year-old mother in my son's class quipped. I smiled.

"I think you mean *experienced*," I replied, possibly with too much snark.

She and I had been chatting about kids and their many activities, but when she learned this was our fifth child to walk through the kindergarten doors, her response was immediate. She quickly recovered with an apologetic, "You must have it all figured out by now!"

Her common response to our big family immediately reminds me of the early days of our sixth baby, Gianna. She was born six days overdue, and the days preceding her birth, I was camped out at the second of three baseball tournaments in a month. Unlike basketball or soccer, baseball games last forever, and my nearly forty-year-old body was feeling it. Of course, the baseball tournament was sandwiched between sports banquets, piano lessons, 4-H project work, religious retreats, school field days, end-of-year everything, and our many volunteer obligations. Gianna was a May baby, and I knew if we could just make it a few more weeks the leisure of summer would be upon us.

It was just a season.

When we arrived home with our new baby, a plumber was fixing two leaky toilets and the kids were boisterous and quite anxious to get to know their new baby sister. Those first few weeks were filled with finding our new rhythm. As a college graduate with two degrees in agriculture, I lovingly refer to it as the 3:3:3 phenomenon (three months, three weeks, three days)—the exact gestation of a litter of piglets. It takes just about 114 days for us to resume semblance of a "normal" schedule after the birth of a baby.

When August came into view, at the end of that 114-day mark, we were hitting our stride; I could feel it. The fall semester started buzzing all around, and we happily enrolled the kids in multiple sports teams, signed them up for piano lessons, joined the school choir, took on more volunteer activities, and began filling up the family calendar. After all, it's what we had been doing for years. A new baby wasn't going to interrupt that well-oiled machine. I was an experienced mom now.

As the activities increased and the strain worsened, I chalked it up to sleep deprivation. While Gianna wasn't a colicky baby, she was up multiple times a night to nurse, and that left me exhausted. Yet everyone expected me to be the overachieving mom—fixing lunches, chauffeuring kids, cleaning house, coordinating school fundraising projects, and managing the schedule, all with a baby on my hip, a Dr Pepper in my hand, and a smartphone in my back pocket. As a type A, get-things-done kind of mom, I was happy to prove everyone right. I could totally do it all, just watch me.

One month later, while catching up on freelance graphic design work in a local coffee shop with just one child, a well-meaning patron stopped to admire Gianna. We exchanged polite nods, and he moved up to his place in line and ordered his fancy-sounding drink. As he retrieved his concoction of caffeine, he stopped by my table again and we began chatting.

It started with, "She's beautiful." But when I shared she was our sixth, without missing a beat he said, "Is her name Oops?" with a slight chuckle, a wink, and a smile. When you have six children, people say the most insensitive things out loud.

However, in that same breath where he chastised our family planning skills, he simultaneously shook his head and murmured, "How do you do it all and not go crazy?" After all, with a brood that big, one should know how to manage all the moving pieces and parts, right?

I politely half smiled and then graciously sprinted for my minivan. The pressure was building, and his comment almost sent me over the edge. There was an adoration chapel nearby, and I found myself parked in front of it a few minutes later. Gianna and I quietly entered. The stained-glass windows were powerful and radiant, as beams of light strewn inside. There was a cloak of peace there, and I could already feel the tears stinging my eyes.

That man's words had cut deep, much deeper than I wanted to admit, but I had no idea what to do with them. For half an hour, I simply sat in that chapel as one tear after another slowly leaked from my eyes. While Gianna nursed and slept contentedly, I stared at the peace in her face and desperately longed to find it myself.

Life was starting to teeter dangerously. So many of my friends had struggled from postpartum depression, and I was always grateful to have skated through that phase with nary a concern. But not this time. I found myself pulled over on the side of the road, nearly hyperventilating and feeling shaky, as I dialed my obstetrician's phone number. The nurse answered, and I froze. With Herculean effort, I managed to squeak out the words, "I . . . am not . . . OK." And then exhaled sharply.

After a long conversation with her and my doctor, we formulated a plan. It was going to require me to be real about my bandwidth and make some drastic changes. I was just desperate enough to try them.

That night, life buzzed all around me. Kids were shouting because homework still wasn't completed, my husband was tapping out emails and text messages on his phone, the shower water was running upstairs, the dishwasher was busily humming in the kitchen, and my head was pounding from it all.

I was a little worried about talking to Scott about all this. He's the master of positivity, and tonight I wanted to shove his positivity where the sun didn't shine because nothing felt right; it all felt like defeat. As soon as the kids were in bed, he sat across from me and with absolutely no warning I blurted out, "I cannot do this anymore."

"Dinner? Homework? Shuttling kids? It's fine, babe," he assured me, "it's just been one of those weeks. It's a season and it will all be over soon."

Nope, it had been one of those *lives*. In this moment, Scott just didn't get the cavernous depth of my anxiety. With a forced smile, I looked at him confidently and with a little defiance said, "The cruise director is tired, sweetheart. Something has to give."

The truth is that I wasn't the only one who was burning out. Our whole family was suffering because we had failed to prioritize. We had children struggling academically, the defiance was growing at an unhealthy rate, and the yelling was reaching decibels even the neighbors could hear. We were so busy doing every-thing, and all we had to show for it was a house in disarray, two stressed-out parents, five overcommitted children, and a screaming baby punctuating it all. My daily dose of Dr Pepper wasn't enough. We needed a serious intervention.

Scott and I held up the mirror to our lives that evening. We asked the hard questions:

- Is this volunteer obligation making our family more holy?
- Did we join this activity because it seemed like the right thing to do or because we wanted to do it?
- Were we pressured to sign up for all these things?

We started assessing all the things, and the ways, in which we had gone wrong, and we decided to start changing things by putting a six-month moratorium on activities—every last one of them. Every sports team, music lesson, social invitation, and volunteer activity got the ax. The only thing that survived the slash and burn was our service to the Church as lectors, altar servers, and extraordinary ministers of Holy Communion.

I know, our friends audibly gasped too.

Then we went public. As we started turning things down, the enablers immediately came to our aid and out of the woodwork. Parents offered to help us shuttle kids to and from track and baseball practice, coaches called to see how they could accommodate our situation, and family members offered to babysit those children left behind. It was humbling to see the community of friends and family rally, but it was also deeply troubling.

Their intentions were so, so good. But do you see? We were all on the crazy bus to burnout city, and yet the road was paved with the best of intentions. In our quest to be perfect parents with the perfectly busy calendar, we didn't want any dissenters because that meant we might actually have to make some hard decisions about where we were spending our time and our money. Nobody wants to be sitting on the bus alone; crazy craves company.

I won't lie, the drastic detox was brutal. Just a few days in, we started second-guessing the sheer lunacy of our plans. The kids kept telling me they were bored, and I was running out of distasteful household tasks like scrubbing toilets and polishing baseboards. Perhaps we should've done a slow fade of removing ourselves from obligations. Affirmation came from the unlikeliest of sources though. One week in, our son who is a gifted athlete and the one we feared would take it the hardest said, "I'm kinda glad I'm not playing baseball. I was feeling stressed out." He was ten.

One of our most important takeaways on that day was that just because we *could* do something didn't mean we *should*.

The following spring rolled around, during our six-month moratorium, and with the Texas bluebonnets in full bloom, we packed up the minivan during spring break and toured the painted churches in Central Texas. They're famous, and for good reason. In the 1800s, Czech and German immigrants made their way to Texas and settled here. They were tight-knit communities named after the places left behind, such as Praha, Schulenburg, and Dubina. But these people missed home and desired for their places of worship to resemble the Gothic structures they once knew. Making do with paint and imagination, they transformed these simple buildings into stunning churches filled with art that is a feast for the eye, the mind, and the soul, and they have been preserved beautifully. (In case you're wondering, the Nativity of Mary, Blessed Virgin Catholic Church in High Hill is a family favorite.)

We decided our children should experience such an expression of art, culture, and history. Five minutes into the expedition they were all screaming about how stupid this was, how boring it would be, and why we couldn't just stop off at the Texas gas station superstore of Buc-ee's instead. As we walked into the first church and I whisper-screamed to my children to be on their best behavior, Scott caught my eye and lovingly said, "I don't think that's working, Kathryn."

With a heavy thud, I plunked myself down in the pew wondering about the ridiculousness of this whole venture. One, was the moratorium really necessary and were the kids even getting the message? Two, why *didn't* we just go to Buc-ee's with its seventy-five bathrooms (no lie) and seventy-nine-cent mega-ounce Dr Peppers instead? The kids could overdose on sugary snacks and barbecue sandwiches while browsing the racks of clothing, home décor, and collegiate goods. But the baby was fussing and needed to be nursed.

The church was packed with visitors, and it had no cry room. I resigned myself to the situation and began nursing as my gaze was lifted upward at the beauty of this German church, amid the paintings of immigrants. The columns are each painted to look like marble, and not in the tacky 1985 faux style done by interior designers either. These were painted with passion, with an eye on heaven. Just as one is taken aback by the beauty and sheer enormity of St. Peter's Basilica in Rome, I was stunned by the attention to detail, the forethought to make something so ordinary, extraordinary. As a Texas gal with German ancestors, this church really spoke to my soul. The colors are vivid; the pews are an old, carved wood, steady and solid. Sitting there, I could almost envision those immigrants happily greeting one another after a hard day's work and finding solace in this space, for it looked, and felt, like home.

Just as I was having this spiritual epiphany, my kids were storming the altar and Scott was rolling his eyes in defeat in the corner. I just smiled. Gianna was perfectly content, with her free hand resting just above my heart. We had finally found our peace. It wasn't quiet and it wasn't orderly and it certainly wasn't Pinterest-perfect, but boy had we landed the intention with a perfect ten. I'm also certain that at the end of that visit, four-sixths of the Whitaker children were in timeout.

Sometimes intention is messy, but this time the authenticity had a holy purpose, and that was our end game. That was the bus I wanted to be on at the end of the day.

Space to rest was becoming a disappearing commodity in our home, and I wanted to change that. Years before, I attended a Cursillo retreat that required participants to be silent for the first twenty-four hours. It was my own personal purgatory. People were smiling and nodding and acting as if this was the greatest thing since the invention of noise-canceling headphones. Me? I was mortified. Didn't these people need interaction, polite dinner conversation, or even a good praise-and-worship song? Where was the music, *any* music? I was so desperate, I escaped to the bathroom and made one of the attendees talk to me. She narrowly escaped and avoided me the rest of the weekend. When the retreat organizers gave us the green light to talk, I felt as if the room finally had life again.

Obviously, that retreat happened early in my parenting career because now, as the mom of six, twenty-four minutes of uninterrupted silence is like buried treasure. Going to the bathroom doesn't even happen without twenty questions around here. My house certainly doesn't resemble a cloistered convent, but it sure didn't need to be a twenty-four-hour Led Zeppelin concert either.

That Cursillo weekend demonstrated, quite effectively, just how much I feared the silence and unscheduled time. When we look at our calendars with blank boxes, we feel the urge to put something in them to flaunt our productivity, if only to ourselves. The question *What did you do today?* haunts us. It certainly did for me. My gravest mistake as a parent has been believing the lie that my worth was measured by my children's accomplishments, our family's list of events and activities, and the accolades that came with it all. I greatly feared my lack of doing, rather than the purposeful act of being. If I didn't have anything tangible to show for my efforts, wouldn't people call me out as a fraud? If asked to choose between sitting down to play Candy Land for ten minutes with the kids or wiping down sticky kitchen walls, my default was always the walls. And I hated myself for it.

But when you define your family culture and prioritize your commitments, it's easier to say no to some things and *hell yes* to those that bring you joy. The challenge of it all, though, is that the nos in our life are often a series of really fantastic and beautiful things. Should we go to that birthday party, parish festival, or funeral visitation? We lament over saying no to any activity, so we say yes to them all and end up not being fully present to anything. We believe we're living full lives, and instead we're just filling them full of stuff—stuff with no purpose and no direction. In the end, does this busyness nurture and feed our family, or is it just sucking the joy right out of us?

Our family feels that pinch a little quicker than most because of sheer numbers. Here, everything is multiplied. But I'm talking about intention. Don't believe the lie that a full calendar means a purpose-filled life.

There is joy in the silence. Early in our marriage, Scott began working for the Archdiocese of Indianapolis in stewardship and development. The archbishop at the time was a Benedictine. Archbishop Buechlin had the gentlest spirit and an overarching sense of peace about him. It's no surprise that his seminary prepara-tions at St. Meinrad were built around a Benedictine philosophy of *otium sanctum,* or holy leisure. It sounds lovely, doesn't it? To me, initially, it sounded like wasted time—that is, until the pressure cooker of always doing had me craving this elusive concept of holy leisure.

In a 2010 homily, Pope Benedict XVI said, "We live in a society in which it seems that every space, every moment must be 'filled' with initiatives, activity, sound; often there is not even time to listen and dialogue. . . . Let us not be afraid to be silent outside and inside our-selves, so that we are able not only to perceive God's voice, but also the voice of the person next to us, the voices of others."

How in the world does an active family of eight, with children from teen to toddler, actually practice stillness?

I'll tell you.

You shift your thinking. Make it as much of a prior-ity in your family as scheduling band camp and soccer tournaments, piano lessons, and ACT prep courses. Almost every saint heard God in the quiet, not on the loudspeaker at a cheer competition. Participating in extracurriculars or volunteering in your community are all good and often holy endeavors as our children learn important skills such as teamwork, time man-agement, goal setting, problem solving, and conflict resolution. But if we desire peace and purpose, we must make room for God's love. How can he shine his light in if we insist he fit into our packed schedules?

This phenomenon of cramming as much as pos-sible into your life, without pausing to identify your purpose, is the premise for Patrick Lencioni's book *The*

3 Big Questions for a Frantic Family. He emphasizes, "We are a passionate family that believes in standing up strongly for what is right, even when there is a cost. We live our lives around our Church and our faith, placing special emphasis on maximizing our involvement in our children's lives, and nurturing family-like relationships with our friends."

Everything does have a cost; you just have to decide what currency you're going to use and how high a price you are willing to pay.

Newsflash: Living a life with purpose and intention will not be popular. Friends may beg you to join the crazy fray once again, or they will sigh and wistfully share that they wish they could live your carefree life, but they are just too busy. Don't get sucked into the lie, y'all. If you are a slave to your life, it's because you *choose* to be.

Leave it to St. Francis de Sales, a sixteenth-century saint, to have advice applicable five centuries later:

> Don't sow your desires in someone else's garden; just cultivate your own as best you can; don't long to be other than what you are, but desire to be thoroughly what you are. Direct your thoughts to being very good at that and to bearing the crosses, little or great, that you will find there. Believe me, this is the most important and least understood point to the spiritual life. We all love according to what is our taste; few people like what is according to their duty or to God's liking. What is the use of building castles in Spain when we have to live in France?

Or, as we say in Texas, don't hang your wash on someone else's line.

Our family learned from our mistakes of overdoing life. We learned that the view from the land of busy isn't all it's cracked up to be. Yes, every once in a while we're tempted to jump back in that lane for a fleeting second. Then we pause, look heavenward, and do a family check. Is this serving God, or is it serving our egos? Are we doing this in the name of "preparing our kids for college applications," or are our motives honest and true?

When the tempers rise or we feel we're spinning out of control, we start saying no again. Or is it *hell yes*? I suppose that depends upon which bus you've chosen.

I found the one whom my soul loves.

★ *Song of Solomon 3:4*

Chapter 10

THE MIRACLE
BUSINESS

Sometimes, you want to tell God to shove it.

Life seemed pretty normal until that twenty-week anatomy scan ultrasound with Luke at the maternal fetal medicine doctor's office in early 2009. After weeks of scans and genetic tests as well as an amniocentesis, my perinatologist suspected a placental tumor was interfering with Luke's growth. But pathology called my placenta "unremarkable." Or as I like to call it, crappy luck. When I delivered at thirty-six weeks, he was the size of a thirty-two-weeker at just a touch over three pounds.

In addition to Luke's small stature, he was diagnosed with a pelvic kidney (his right kidney sits unprotected in his pelvis). It meant we simply gained a nephrologist and that Luke's days in the NICU were

meant to be "feeder-grower"—we would get him gain-
ing weight, regulating his own body temperature, and
eating independently. On day nine, that all went out
the window when I opened his diaper and found it
was filled with blood. He had contracted necrotizing
enterocolitis—a serious intestinal illness that was eating
away at his intestines, killing them as it moved through
his bowel. It's what caused him to code and have to
be resuscitated. Hours later, he endured his first emergency bowel surgery, the one where he had a two in
ten chance of surviving. Then came the onslaught of
abnormalities with multiple major organs. Over the
course of his first year, Luke underwent an additional
four surgeries—two emergency ones to the bowel, one
to correct his tethered spinal cord, and one to implant
ear tubes. At age two, the cardiologist closed a hole in
his heart, and at age four we closed his encephalocele
(a neural tube defect in his brain). Plus, we had numerous hospitalizations due to infection, bowel issues, and
life-threatening reactions to medications.

At one point, Luke had thirteen different specialists
that focused on his brain, spine, gut, kidney, heart, ears,
feet, genetics, blood, cognitive development, speech,
physical movement, and feeding, in addition to his regular pediatrician and a general surgeon—a grand total
of fifteen. It was so intense that at a physical medicine
appointment, the doctor looked at me after I rattled off
Luke's various anomalies and said, "Do you have a job
in the medical field?"

The mom who had once almost fainted at the sight
of a nurse starting an IV on her preemie now helped
show nursing students how to insert an NG tube and
care for an ostomy. It's OK, those terms used to be

foreign to me too. I became a student of how to best care for Luke. If I couldn't fix him, then I could be damn sure I was his best advocate by educating myself on all of his challenges and how to overcome them.

For months after our initial NICU discharge, the faces and cries of the mothers who walked out of the hospital with empty arms haunted me. I would cry myself to sleep feeling grateful we graduated from NICU hell yet feeling the guilt of survival. It was real and it was painful. Time, and its healing, became my constant companion.

I figured I could either sit in a closet and cry all day or be the strong, southern woman I knew I could be, shake the dust off my boots, and move forward. Luke and his siblings taught me that not everything is a spiritual epiphany. Sometimes you just get up and move forward because it's what you have to do.

Weeks turned to months and months to years. We began to pull ourselves from the vortex of Dell Children's hospital stays and specialist visits. Our new normal began to emerge, and I was handling developmental setbacks better, parenting with a bit more grace, flourishing in my marriage and in my personal self-care.

Three years after his birth, during one of Luke's developmental pediatrician visits, we ran the circuit of specialists asking them what they thought about a future pregnancy. Could this happen again? Was it hereditary or just really crappy luck? The developmental pediatrician, upon hearing the news we were considering having another baby, reassured us that even if having another baby was a leap of faith, she was our biggest supporter. "The world needs more Whitakers," she said with a beaming smile. The hematologist shared, "God didn't lead you astray on this one. He held you through it all." She mentioned that talking about her faith with us was a rarity in her profession and she was grateful for the opportunity. Her husband was one of Luke's two cardiologists, and he echoed her sentiments. In fact, every specialist was in our cheering section.

While I didn't need their permission, having the support (and in many cases, prayers) of so many pediatric specialists and therapists was a boon to my soul. They had weathered so much of this story right alongside us. They, more than anyone else, knew the depth and breadth of our medical journey.

We leaned into the support from all those specialists, but not before praying a nine-day novena to St. Thérèse of Lisieux. Novenas are a bit like asking your best friend to pray for an intention for nine consecutive days. I had really warmed to St. Thérèse during the early days of my pregnancy with Luke, so it seemed logical to ask her to intercede as we prayed about adding another baby to our family. St. Thérèse often sends roses as a sign of answered prayer during those nine days.

Our intention was clear—we wanted to add another child to our family, even though there was no guaranteed "normal pregnancy." We knew that if God allowed the crazy, he would also send the grace.

We began our prayer with great hope and joy but kept the intention between God and Scott and me. Four days after we began the novena, we had a last-minute cancellation by friends who were accompanying us to a Catholic schools dinner. We reached out to another couple, and they joyfully accompanied us, but not without handing us a gift bag filled with a token of their appreciation—a primrose.

God and Thérèse were already looking like quite the show-offs, but on day nine, our final day of prayers, they really went big. Each January, our school hosts a eucharistic procession. The priest processes through the halls with the monstrance (an ornate receptacle that displays the consecrated Host we believe is Jesus), guided by the eighth-grade class. They drop rose petals in front of the priest as he walks. But because our principal is allergic to roses, the students quickly collect them before she returns. I was unable to attend the procession that year, but my girls were enthusiastically telling us about it at suppertime. Scott looked at me and said, "Just because they're talking about roses doesn't mean St. Thérèse is affirming our intention."

Then Clare exclaimed, "Oh wait, Dad, I'll show you!" She and Anna-Laura returned to the kitchen table, turned out their backpacks, and dropped hundreds of rose petals across our table.

A few months later, the pregnancy test came back positive.

My pregnancy with our sixth baby was nothing short of miraculous—it was textbook normal. At twenty weeks gestation, we were back at the same maternal fetal medicine doctor's office that had diagnosed Luke's pregnancy with unlikely viability. This time, however, the mood was markedly different. Our perinatologist walked in the room, smiled, and gave us a huge hug. Not only was he congratulating us on a perfectly normal pregnancy but also he got to fist-bump Luke—his miracle story. He delivers difficult and sometimes devastating news to parents every day in his profession.

But on this day, he saw the fruits of his specialty—magnificent doesn't come close to describing it.

All along I prayed for a full-term pregnancy. I went into labor six days past my due date. Be careful what you pray for—you just might get it.

With Luke, just days after I delivered him, my obstetrician gently held my hand and told me if we ever tried for another baby, I would be an excellent candidate for VBAC (vaginal birth after Caesarean). I heeded her advice with this baby and went into the experience with confidence in my body. While the five previous deliveries had been aided by an epidural, I decided to birth completely natural (with no pain medication) with this baby.

Scott and I arrived at the hospital ready to greet this new life in typical sassy Kathryn style. I let the nurse know I was passing on birthing in a hospital gown; instead, I wore my nursing tank and a knit skirt, with flip-flops. While I allowed them to start an IV, we capped it so I wasn't tethered to an IV pole. They had the access they wanted, and I had the freedom to move around. I even put in my fancy earrings because when it's your leap-of-faith baby, you call the shots. At 6:00 a.m., I already had quite the reputation in the labor and delivery unit as "that mom"—the one who wore her own clothes during labor, who kept the baby's gender a surprise, and who was naturally birthing her sixth baby.

Through God's grace, he gifted me a labor and delivery nurse who knew just how to push me (no pun intended) into furthering the labor naturally, and she fully appreciated my sarcasm.

When my labor stalled, Sharon walked in the room and said, "Kathryn, it's time to get serious about delivering this baby." Pitocin wasn't an option because of my previous C-section as it put too much strain on the uterus, increasing the likelihood of a uterine rupture. Um, no thanks.

We cleared the room, and with encouragement from Scott, we began dancing to the Ann Arbor Dominican album *Mater Eucharistiae*. I had asked for prayer intentions from friends and family, and with each contraction, I offered up another prayer. The music, the intentions, and the steady arms of Scott embracing me finally allowed me to fall into the miracle of God's perfect plan for this birth.

I finally let it all go.

Three hours later, amid a room full of nurses, a birth photographer, and my obstetrician, I gave birth to Gianna Thérèse without the aid of pain medication. It was the most spiritually intense experience of my life. Our daughter was named for a brave mother and physician, St. Gianna Molla, who chose life, and Thérèse for the saint that walked us all the way through hell and back.

Life rarely hits autopilot though. That cruising altitude never seems to last for long.

At six weeks, just after nursing Gianna, I noticed a slight arch in her back and her eyes roll back. The first time it happened, I dismissed it. When it happened again the following morning, I panicked. It sure looked like a seizure. With no more recurrences that afternoon, I sent the kids and Scott off to Mass while I finished nursing her, assuring them I would join them late. Fifteen minutes later, she seized again. That did it. I packed her up in the minivan, sped to the emergency room, and called Scott on the way. What was normally a twenty-minute drive, I made in ten.

I am no stranger to emergency rooms. When you pair "newborn" with "seizure" at the ER check-in, they whisk you right back for observation. She seized again when I pulled her from the car seat, this time under the watchful eyes of a nurse and a resident. That got us a first-class ticket to the neurosurgery wing on the fourth floor. Scott got the other five children settled back home and joined me a few hours later at the hospital.

Once again, God laid out one providential miracle after another. Even though I sat in Dell Children's with a baby who had no answers, because of Luke, I knew a neurosurgeon who did. Once again, my friend Angela (the same one who encouraged me to go to marriage counseling) arrived at Gianna's bedside just before I fell apart. Once again, a Dominican sister appeared at the door when I begged God for some holy backup. Once again, our community of friends rallied to help. And once again, God entered the room and filled me with hope.

For six months, we slowly watched our baby's seizures subside. At six months, they ceased to exist, and they have never returned.

Gianna healed us in ways we didn't know we needed to be healed. With her came a new season of parenthood. We took the lessons of Luke, along with the resiliency of our other children, and began implementing them with her in every aspect of our life—intentional prayer, priestly relationships, digital life, marriage, holy friendships, joy and order, family vacations, self-care, and family culture.

A few years after giving birth to her, I was preparing for a talk at a local mother's group. A Dominican sister had gifted me this prayer on a worn piece of paper several years prior. As I was rummaging through my Bible—stuffed with prayer cards, intention lists, and bookmarks—"Your Cross" by St. Francis de Sales literally fell in my lap.

> The everlasting God has in His wisdom foreseen from eternity the cross that He now presents to you as a gift from His inmost heart. This cross He now sends you He has considered with His all-knowing eyes, understood with His divine mind, tested with His wise justice, warmed with loving arms and weighed with His own hands to see that it be not one inch too large and not one ounce too heavy for you. He has blessed it with His holy Name, anointed it with His consolation, taken one last glance at you and your courage, and then sent it to you from heaven, a special greeting from God to you, an alms of the all-merciful love of God.

St. Francis de Sales, the patron saint of writers, was a voracious evangelist—a sixteenth-century high achiever for Jesus. He weathered the tempers and impatience of those who refused to hear the beauty of God's message of love, rarely growing weary.

Until I began writing this book, this prayer was all I knew of him. The more I learn about his zest for evangelization and seemingly inhuman level of patience for God's mission for him, I am humbled. He believed lay people had a mission and a calling to live a life of holiness within their vocation, no matter how messy their life may be. Whatever your vocation may be, live it and love it, *without apology.*

For many of us, we mistakenly believe that once God has gifted us with "our cross"—a medical diagnosis, a failing marriage, a job loss, death of a loved one, or something else heavy and hard—there won't be others to carry.

I used to believe that. But the lessons of Luke, how my other children adapted and changed, and the redemption of Gianna showed me perhaps the most important lesson of all.

The miracle business is bigger than we think.

Yes, God performs big and grand miracles. But what about the everyday miracles, thick in the mess of life? God opened our eyes to them all.

I truly believe I'll be unpacking the lessons of Luke's birth and its effect on our family for a lifetime. I rarely look at a situation the same because of how God continues to transform our lives. And with each lesson, no matter how hard or easy it is, I have gratitude.

I can almost hear Colbert shouting *Yee-haw*! I finally learned to love the bomb.

My friend Donna was right when she shared with me, "Luke Whitaker: one of God's reminders that he's still in the miracle business."

God knew how to reach the deepest recesses of my heart—with a tiny three-pound baby. Your miracle may look different, but don't discount the gift of surrender. It's where intimacy thrives and you are transformed.

I am not perfect—far from it, y'all. But I am better.

In high school, I was part of the handbell choir at the Disciples of Christ church. My handbell teacher was a gifted musician (who later played the organ at my Catholic wedding), and she always pushed us to play our best. "Perform like you practice," she would often say. At the conclusion of each Wednesday-night practice session, Judy would have us close our eyes and recite the words from Isaiah: "They that wait upon the Lord shall renew their strength. They shall mount up with wings as eagles. They shall run and not be weary. They shall walk and not faint" (Isaiah 40:31, KJV).

I lost count of how many times I have recited that scripture in my life. The intense love of the Word of God has been one of the most resplendent things I took from my formative days as a Protestant.

Life is just one long practice, where we make mistakes and start from the beginning of the music sheet again. We have a teacher there, guiding and encouraging us. But we're human, and sometimes the mistakes and crosses of life make us feel we're unworthy. We forget that God is in the miracle business every day.

When show time comes for you, don't panic and run off the stage. I hope you remember how to let God love you through, and in, the mess.

Bob Goff, author of *Love Does* and the champion of big love, reminds us, "We get to decide what we'll give to the world and what we'll take from it, Love big; pack light."

This life was meant for living, so I encourage you to set fear aside and love bigger. Can I get a *hell yes*? Let's say it a little louder for the folks in the back, shall we?

ACKNOWLEDGMENTS

Books don't write themselves, and they certainly aren't written by just one person. Many of my dear friends and the stories we share are on these pages. I am grateful for their witness and their vast influence on my life. I am a better writer because they encouraged me to see life through a different lens.

Fr. Dave Dwyer, those were happy tears I cried when you said *yes* to writing the foreword. Your laugh (it is *the* best), encouragement, and witness to our family are such a joy. We may argue over the occasional Pantone color, but we always agree on barbecue, Jesus, and queso—as it should be. You have been my cheerleader long before a book was ever on the horizon, and I love you for that. *Thank you* won't ever be enough.

Jaymie, editor extraordinaire, this book happened because you believed in me. I guess, deep down, that's all I needed. Thank you for making me answer the hard questions even when I didn't want to. The entire team at Ave Maria Press was phenomenal—and I mean that. It was a gift to be co-conspirators in God's plan.

If faith is a journey, then my stints in multiple church communities sure made it even better. To my friends in Indiana at St. Maria Goretti and Our Lady of Mt. Carmel, and at our Texas parishes, St. Elizabeth, St. Theresa, and St. Vincent de Paul, you formed me into a more faithful Catholic. And to each of my Protestant communities—Methodist, Baptist, Nazarene, Disciples of Christ, and every nondenominational Bible church in between—the fervor of your faith showed me how to have a real and lasting relationship with Jesus. I treasure it all.

About halfway through writing I realized other people besides my husband might actually read this book. And then I panicked. God led me to the "just right" people to review various chapters. Their feedback, while I expected it to be something like, *This is crap!* was actually supportive, challenging, and candid. My work here is markedly better because of them. Thanks for being so refreshingly honest Cindy Todd; Leigh Ann Torres; Kelli Kelley; Jenny Uebbing; Sr. Maria Fatima, O.P.; Fr. Tom Reitmeyer; Samantha Skaggs; Stephanie Weinert; and Bonnie Engstrom.

Mary and Jerry Lenaburg, there would be no book—truly—if not for you both. Mary, thank you for speaking truth and telling me to dig out my big girl undies and just write the dadgum book. It's been awesome sharing this experience with you. Nobody can GIF text quite like you can. Jerry, I owe you some TX Whiskey and a plateful of barbecue for putting up with it all.

Jennifer Fulwiler, Rachel Balducci, Brandon Vogt, Michele Faehnle, Marika Flatt, Denise Aziz, and Danielle Bean, thank you for being so generous with your advice; you have no idea how much it helped.

To my tribe of prayer warriors—y'all know who you are—how is it that I can be so blessed with holy and faithful women? My sweet tea pitcher is ready for you!

The love and support of my parents, brother, mother-in-law, brother-in-law, and sisters-in-law has always been there and what a buoy it was. The lessons I've learned from you have strengthened my faith and reminded me of the power of love and how grand God's mercy really is.

Kathryn Whitaker is a Catholic author, blogger, speaker, and freelance graphic designer. A sixth-generation Texan, she was raised as an evangelical Protestant. She met her husband on a blind date at Texas A&M and on the eve of their wedding, Whitaker converted to Catholicism and never looked back.

Since 2007, Whitaker has shared on her blog—with honesty, authenticity, and a healthy dose of sass—what it's like raising a raucous Catholic family, including a preemie, while balancing her freelance graphic design business and her love of the Aggies, keeping her obsession with the Container Store in check, and stocking the fridge with plenty of Dr Pepper.

Whitaker has contributed to *Blessed Is She*, *Take Up and Read*, *ATX Catholic*, and Hand to Hold's preemie blog. She has appeared in *USA Today*, Iowa Catholic Radio, *The Son Rise Morning Show*, Relevant Radio, and is a regular guest on *The Jennifer Fulwiler Show* on SiriusXM.

Kathryn and her husband, Scott, live with their family in Austin, Texas.

teamwhitaker.org
Facebook: TeamWhitaker
Twitter: @kwhitaker96
Instagram: kwhitaker96
Pinterest: kwhitaker96

Fr. Dave Dwyer, C.S.P., is executive director of Busted Halo ministries, host of the *Busted Halo Show* on SiriusXM's The Catholic Channel, and cohosts *Conversations with Cardinal Dolan*, which also airs on The Catholic Channel and on multiple television stations.

There is only one regret I carry with this book, and it is that I didn't get it written before my grandfather passed away. I hear they have a glorious library in heaven, Papa.

Before I signed on the dotted line to begin writing, Scott and I shared the news with our six children. Without hesitation they said, "You should do it, Mom." And so I did. Will, John Paul, Anna-Laura, Clare, Luke, and Gianna—I wrote this book for you so you could see how big and wide God's love has been, and continues to be, for our family. You make me grateful for this mom gig every day, even on the hard ones.

Scott, this is as much your book as it is mine. We did it together. You kept the house running—the kids might argue you do it much better than me—while I wrote like crazy. You were the first reader for every chapter, making notes in the sidebar. *Nobody cares!* and *What are you saying here?* were some of my favorites. I trusted you with my heart, and in turn, you pushed me to dig a little deeper. Writing this book only made me love you more. It's over! Let's go grab some queso and Shiner.